BRITISH RAILWAY
FIRST GENERATION DMUs

for the Modeller and Historian

Stuart Mackay

Ian Allan
PUBLISHING

First published 2006

ISBN (10) 0 7110 3156 8
ISBN (13) 978 0 7110 3156 2

Published by Ian Allan Publishing

an imprint of Ian Allan Publishing Ltd, Hersham, Surrey KT12 4RG.
Printed in England by Ian Allan Printing Ltd, Hersham, Surrey KT12 4RG.

Code: 0611/C

Visit the Ian Allan Publishing website at www.ianallanpublishing.com

CONTENTS

Front cover, top:
Birmingham's first regular DMU service started on 5 March 1956, running from New Street to Lichfield City. Based at Monument Lane, the Derby Lightweight power/trailer sets provided ten more southbound and 11 additional northbound services than previously. Also, with journey times reduced by two to six minutes, the first week of traffic saw 40,000 passengers carried, compared with 12,000 in the same week of the previous year. Some services terminated at Four Oaks, where these two sets are seen on 11 March 1956. Vehicles allocated to the line initially were Nos M79121-79134/M79642-79655 and M79143-79149/M79663-79669, although some of these were on loan from North Wales and other sets were drafted in from time to time to help cope with growing passenger numbers. An early victim of the desire to standardise coupling codes to ensure compatibility, the Lightweights were replaced on the line by Met-Camms from the summer timetable, and they moved to Manchester. *Colour-Rail*

Front cover, bottom:
Cravens-built No E50364 of set No 48 is seen at Manningtree in September 1977. All the four-lamp versions were built for the NER's dieselisation of Hull, the batch containing 14 Leyland-engined and 17 AEC-engined vehicles. The centre of the cab front has been repaired. *Colour-Rail*

Back cover:
Not all Class 128s had the gangways removed and plated over; No 55992 still has its gangways in place in this view at Reading MPD on 20 February 1988, where it is seen with No 54280, the pair having worked from Doncaster that day. Although the gangway remains, the headcode boxes have been removed and replaced by marker lights. There is a removable panel under the driver's window to enable access to the back of the driver's desk. The last five cars were withdrawn in 1990, and none survives. *Mel Holley*

Title page:
Former GWR vehicles surviving into the British Railways DMU era, and painted to match, Nos W33W and W38W are seen with an intermediate car, converted from Hauled stock, passing over the water troughs at Aldermaston, forming the 12.37 Newbury–Reading in August 1959. These are the pre-1950s vehicles that came closest to the first-generation units. *G. H. Hunt/Colour-Rail DE1669*

INTRODUCTION

As this book is in the 'Modeller and Historian' series, the selection of photographs and the information given in the captions should be of interest and help for such readers. A number of views of centre cars and the rear ends of vehicles are included, which are not normally published but are full of useful details. I have also highlighted items that make identification of types possible.

Telling the full story of first-generation DMUs in one volume is no easy task, as within the space available this must cover the 50-year history of over 30 types, nearly 4,000 vehicles, countless different liveries and many variations. For this reason it was decided not to feature some vehicles that other books usually include, namely the DEMUs and the four-wheeled railbuses. I have also restricted the period covered to just enter the early 1990s as the number of liveries that have appeared since then would fill half the book. As the railcar story is not finished yet on the national network this leaves potential for a further volume. It has been deliberate policy not to include too many of the early blue livery variations, which I have a liking for myself (I may even have influenced a few of these now in preservation!), and would have happily added an example for each class, but this would not have given a balanced representation of the blue era.

Thanks are due to all the photographers who have helped me, especially Ron White at Colour-Rail on whom I have perhaps relied upon too much, but who has always been more than helpful. Thanks also to Steve Huson for the engine photographs, and to John Horne and Kevin Dowd for checking the text. The biggest thanks however, goes to all the people who have contributed information over the years to the Railcar website, making it an excellent resource for information and a place where readers can find out more if they desire. Although the greatest care has been given in ensuring accuracy, please don't hesitate to submit anything you want to challenge, via the publishers!

Stuart Mackay
www.railcar.co.uk

BRITISH RAILWAYS FIRST-GENERATION DIESEL MULTIPLE-UNITS

In the pre-Nationalisation years the various railway companies experimented with diesel-engined railcars in various forms, but with no real success, except the GWR. In 1949, the Railway Executive set up a 'Committee on Types of Motive Power' whose remit was to look at the advantages of steam, electric, diesel-electric, diesel-mechanical and gas turbine traction from an economic viewpoint. Not much evolved on the railcar front at first, but communications from two private firms (Metropolitan Ganz and ACV) prompted the Railway Executive to call them to re-examine the scope for the development of diesel railcars.

The Committee agreed that 'It was going to be difficult for British Railways to stand aside from the development of diesel rail-car services since all other railway administrations have devoted a considerable amount of attention to this question', and so the 'Light Weight Trains Committee' was born.

This all-region committee held its first meeting in September 1951, and their remit was to consider and report on the future scope for the employment of lightweight trains; this to include recommendations on areas considered desirable for experiment on an appropriate scale. It applied to main lines, secondary lines and branch lines and covered all types of lightweight units. Their findings led to an announcement in

September 1952 that £500,000 was to be spent on introducing eight diesel railcar sets to the West Riding of Yorkshire for evaluation. However, the intention of learning from these trials fell by the wayside pretty quickly, as many more vehicles were ordered before these were even delivered.

Derby Carriage & Wagon Works was given the task of designing and building these first sets, which had a press launch in April 1954. Immediately praised for their attractive design, the unobstructed view of the line ahead and behind, and for the provision of luggage racks and toilets, they were also criticised for the lack of compartments, the bus-type seats, the absence of arm rests in the third-class areas, and the height of the seats and head rests — which spoilt the view! Mainland Britain's first diesel multiple-unit entered traffic on 14 June 1954, between Leeds and Bradford.

What made these vehicles different from earlier railcars was their ability to work in multiple, allowing the self-contained train to be marshalled into any length (up to a limit) and only requiring one driver to man it, having full control of every power car from the leading cab. Throttle, gears and direction were all electro-pneumatically (EP) controlled — the cab controls being wired to electric valves on each vehicle which allowed compressed air to pass to and operate these three functions. The use of electrics rather than just air allowed easy and quick control of vehicles through the train. The electrical connections between cars, not just between vehicles in a unit, but also

Above: Never really considered as part of the first-generation fleet, but there is no real reason why they should not be. Associated Commercial Vehicles (ACV) built a three-car demonstration train in 1952 which could operate as a one-, two- or three-car set, by virtue of the multiple control system which used jumpers between vehicles. This was the forerunner of the system used on the vehicles in this book; it was effectively ACV that designed and supplied this to both Ireland and the builders of the first-generation fleet. The vehicles ran trials on many branches throughout the country before being taken into British Railways stock and a further eight cars built. Three vehicles are seen leaving Watford carriage shed in preparation for a run to St Albans. They were withdrawn in 1959. *T. Marsh/Colour-Rail DE1668*

with any other vehicles or units that were added to the formation, gave the diesel trains what they needed to succeed.

By the time the first sets entered traffic, Derby already had a commitment to build many more sets. Most of British Railways' own workshops were at full capacity, so a batch was put out to tender, resulting in Metropolitan-Cammell getting an order for 36 sets. This firm went on to build many more, and when the Modernisation Plan was announced several months later, all firms that had originally quoted also received orders.

Two firms, Leyland and AEC, were the biggest commercial road vehicle builders in the UK, and they had a joint venture called BUT — British

United Traction — which produced items such as trolleybuses. They saw the potential of diesel trains and set up a rail division, offering the best equipment from each company, and others, which gave railcar builders an easy option to take when designing units. By using BUT parts in nearly every DMU vehicle built it gave them greater compatibility and played a major part in their success.

An important consideration when units were being introduced was maintenance. The environment required for steam and diesel maintenance was very different, and many railcar components could not be sensibly overhauled or repaired in the soot and grime of steam sheds. Depots had to have areas converted, or new facilities were built. Maintenance staff had to be trained in the new technology, and this was originally done by sending them to the component manufacturers, such as AEC at Southall, Self Changing Gears at Coventry, or to one of the new diesel training schools that emerged. Soon, 'Diesel Instruction Trains' were created and began touring the various depots and training staff on site. These contained a model room full of sectional components with explanations of workings, and a cinema coach for screening technical films.

When introduced, diesel units were generally a huge success. As an example, within a year, receipts on the West Riding line rose by 38%, and continued to rise. Five years later they had risen a staggering 411%. This success was immediately apparent, giving British Railways the confidence to forge ahead with further orders. In December 1954, just five months after the first introductions, the construction of 1,400 vehicles was authorised, at a cost of £17.5 million. It is notable that this huge investment was some months ahead of the 1955 Modernisation Plan!

The well-documented Modernisation Plan envisaged some 4,600 diesel multiple-unit vehicles (including DEMUs, 'Blue Pullmans' and four-wheeled railbuses). Despite the outstanding

success of the vehicles already in traffic, it was not enough to halt the decline of the rail network. The battle against increasing competition from road vehicles was being lost in many areas and line closures meant a review of orders. In the end, 4,171 vehicles were built, 3,810 of which were for diesel multiple-units, by the builders identified below.

Builder	Number of vehicles
British Railways Derby Works	1,392
Metropolitan-Cammell	760
Birmingham Railway Carriage & Wagon	437
British Railways Swindon Works	417
Cravens	405
Gloucester Railway Carriage & Wagon	200
Pressed Steel	149
Park Royal	40
Wickham	10

In the 1970s, AEC was taken over by Leyland, its former BUT partner, which subsequently stopped producing AEC spares. This forced BR to re-engine the AEC-powered vehicles that had a long life expectancy, with the Leyland 680. Latterly, variants of the 680, including the turbocharged TL11, were fitted in some vehicles.

Three types of DMU had hydraulic transmission: the West Riding Derby Lightweights, half of the Cravens single-engined cars (Class 113), and the Derby quad sets for the St Pancras–Bedford line ('127s'). All had direct drive above a certain speed. The remainder used mechanical transmission with a fluid flywheel on the engine acting as an automatic clutch. This drove the gearbox through a freewheel that protected the engine from being reverse driven. The gearboxes were the Wilson epicyclic type with four speeds, fourth being a 1:1 ratio. A cardan shaft connected the gearbox (or torque converters on hydraulic cars), to the final drive, which was an axle-mounted reversing gearbox for forward and reverse control. Heavy-duty

Above left: It was a strange twist that it was the same road technology developments that created the engines and gearboxes etc to make the railcars possible, that also powered their competition. All the railcars used underframe-mounted horizontal engines, and generally, two engines per power car. The first vehicles for the West Riding used 125hp Leyland 600 engines with Leyland Lysholm Smith torque converters. This was considered an unusual choice at the time as it was already considered outdated in road use. Before the next lightweight vehicles were built, a 150hp engine became available, the AEC 220. The mountings and auxiliaries used with this were taken directly from those used on buses, such as the Regal Mark IV, even down to the screw lifting gear for easy engine removal and fitting. The remainder of the 79xxx fleet was fitted with this engine and mounting system (pictured).

Above: All other builds of 150hp vehicles had BUT engines of either 'A' or 'L' type. The 'A' was again the AEC 220, the 'L' was the Leyland 680, a new 150hp version of the earlier-used 600. The mounting system was redesigned, this being identical to both types making them totally interchangeable, although in practice they kept the same type and were not swapped until later re-engining programmes occurred. The 'L' type is pictured.

gearboxes and final drives were used with the more powerful engines.

Ireland had created diesel railcars by converting old locomotive-hauled coaching stock, but British Railways decided to design new vehicles from scratch. Traditionally, railway carriages had all the strength in the underframe, being a self-supporting structure on its own, which was achieved through the use of trusses. The new railcar vehicles were designed to eliminate trussing in order to give unrestricted use of the underframe space, and this was

achieved by combining the underframe and body into an integral structure. This was tackled in different ways by different builders, some more successfully than others. The alloy Derby Lightweights had to have strengthening work done, adding substantial plates to the framework above doorways. It was reported that Class 116 doors became more difficult to open as more passengers boarded the vehicles. In later days, some vehicles, such as the Class 126s, developed noticeable sags along their lengths. There were two lengths of vehicles built, 57ft and 64ft, the choice of which was determined by the route and services the trains were to operate.

The Derby Lightweight bodies were constructed completely of alloy, a choice made on weight terms and concerns over steel availability at the time. Problems with headstock damage after the slightest incidents saw these replaced with steel sections. The Met-Camm 79xxx series sets were known as Met-Camm Lightweights, but were actually steel vehicles with an alloy central roof section, as were all further Met-Camm vehicles. BR was impressed with the Met-Camm cab so redesigned theirs in a similar manner for all subsequent builds. When further alloy cars were built at Derby the redesigned steel cab was used, as well as steel inner ends. All other Derby vehicles were of steel construction, as were all Swindon vehicles, with the exception of the cabs on the Trans-Pennine sets which were a one-piece glass-fibre moulding. All the other private builds were of steel construction except the Wickham cars, which had alloy body panels on a steel frame, while some had alloy roofs.

Alloy vehicles had a much higher initial cost, but needed very little maintenance; steel was cheaper, but called for constant repair because of corrosion. Many steel vehicles soon had alloy strips added to the edges of panels at doorways, which were found to be a corrosion hot-point, and these also reduced water ingress. The method of flush-glazing the bodyside lights (such as on the '104s' where the

glass is clamped to the steel panel by timber), proved to be a corrosion problem, as it was on hauled-stock, and a change was made in new builds to using alloy window frames.

The first Derby cars had alloy roof domes. These had to be hand beaten to shape, which proved very labour intensive, so a switch was made to a glass-fibre moulding, often produced in white which created the white cab roof dome. The Derby Lightweights had these at both ends of the vehicle, the gangway ends being angled the same as the front, so that if the railcar proved to be a failure, a gangway could have been fitted to the cab end and they would then be used as hauled stock!

Another choice over low initial cost or low maintenance was the vehicle's battery cells. Lead-acids were cheap but had a limited life, Ni-Cads were expensive but could take a lot of misuse and had a much longer life span. Both types were used in different classes. The charging system was initially by dynamo, some 79xxx cars having small ones mounted on the rear of the engines, but more commonly there was a large one mounted near or on the bogies and belt-driven by the gearbox output shaft, or axle-driven on unpowered vehicles. Dynamos had the disadvantage of not operating until speed was above approximately 19mph, and later power cars were built with two alternators, belt-driven from the gearbox input, so that they were almost constantly charging. Later, many dynamo cars were converted to alternators.

Not all vehicles had the same control system, so a coupling code symbol was generally applied on the four corners of the vehicle, beside the jumper sockets. They were also sometimes applied to the jumper plugs and sockets themselves. The first eight Derby Lightweight sets for the West Riding had unique underframe components and a different wiring system, and were coded Red Triangle. The remainder of the Derby Lightweights, the Met-Camm 79xxx vehicles, and the three Cravens parcels cars were Yellow Diamond vehicles. The leading power

Above left: Rolls-Royce produced 180hp horizontal engines suitable for railcar use. Some of these were fitted to the Met-Camm units for evaluation, and were subsequently used in the 57ft vehicles that became Classes 110 and 111. A larger, 238hp version (pictured) soon became available and, again after trials, it was used in the 64ft vehicles which became Classes 125 and 127 (both with hydraulic transmission), and in the single-engined (57ft) Cravens cars.

Above: A larger BUT engine became available later — the Leyland Albion 900, originally rated at 230hp but soon derated to 200hp. It was first fitted to the Derby 'Heavyweights' (Class 114) after their 150hp engines proved underpowered, and was subsequently used in other 64ft vehicles, which became Classes 115, 123, 124 and 128.

car's batteries operated the EP valves on remote vehicles, but problems with voltage drop in long formations (there could be up to four power cars maximum, or eight vehicles) saw relays introduced for the Blue Square system. This was more effective as a smaller current was required to operate the relays, which connected the remote vehicle's own power to operate the actual EP valves. A new design of throttle motor was used which gave a smoother control of engine speed, but unfortunately this, and the switching of polarities in many control systems, meant that the conversion of the Yellow Diamond cars to Blue Square was uneconomical. The Orange Star system (Class 125) used a pneumatic throttle system. The White Circle code was applied to two batches of Class 126 Swindon vehicles: the first used the Yellow Diamond system and components with some relays, the second used Blue Square components and was wired as such, other than the order of the circuits at the jumper sockets! The Red Triangle code was re-used by the Class 127s although this was simply a rebranding to prevent hydraulic and gearbox cars being used together. There was also a variant of the Blue Square used from time to time — a diagonal cream line identifying that the vehicle had some minor differences.

Line closures continued through the 1960s, resulting in units becoming surplus. Cascading allowed the withdrawal of the non-standard Red Triangle and Yellow Diamond cars due to a surplus of other 57ft low-density cars. The White Circle and Orange Square units were protected by being specialist types working dedicated services where compatibility was not an issue.

The vehicles were designed for a lifespan of about 20 years, but in the mid-1970s, with no replacements available, a refurbishment programme was started. It was planned to treat 1,800 vehicles, the original selection being those identified as remaining in traffic after 1981. In general, the vehicles had the interiors revamped: new wall panelling, seat coverings and linoleum; fluorescent lighting replaced tungsten, and toilets were updated. Work was also undertaken to improve the heating system, exhausts and engine mounts. However, the work done varied on different vehicles because not all changes were necessarily made.

Class numbers were formally introduced in 1973, under TOPS, Total Operations Processing System, to aid identification. It is widely recognised that numbers had been allocated to some types withdrawn before that date and have been used in this book, such as the Wickham sets as '109s' and the Cravens single-engined power twins as '112' (mechanical) and '113' (hydraulic transmission). As some Swindon 79xxx cars moved to Ayr after Edinburgh–Glasgow services ended, they remained in traffic long enough to become the only 79xxx numbered cars to receive a class number (126).

Initially, each vehicle type within a class received its own code: power cars were 100 to 131 (Classes 130 and 131 were '116' and '122' parcels conversions); driving trailers 140 to 150; centre cars 160 to 190. Power cars were also given sub-classes if required. In general, DMC vehicles would become 1xx/1, and DMBSs 1xx/2, etc. These class numbers are detailed for each type in the relevant section. It was also thought relevant to split classes depending on engine types: '101' and '102' for Met-Camms, '105' and '106' for Cravens, with '101/105s' having AECs and '102/106s' with Leylands.

In 1979, all driving trailers and centre cars received the same class numbers as their power cars and sub classes were dropped, as was the split based on engine type. Class numbers are an easy way of identifying vehicle lengths: '100-113s' and '129s' were 57ft and '114-128s' were 64ft.

Blue asbestos insulation was used in many DMU types, including on the inside of roofs, walls and floors, which were often sprayed with a limpet mixture. A stripping process was started in the late Seventies, often when vehicles were refurbished, but it was an expensive process involving the complete removal of internal panelling in controlled environments and, as the limpet mix comprised asbestos and glue to make it stick, it was a laborious process to remove every last fibre to make the vehicle safe. Many vehicles were not stripped and instead, faced early withdrawal.

It may come as a surprise to learn that the roof vents on vehicles rarely lined up with the ceiling vents inside. This allowed air to circulate around under the roof to prevent condensation, but also meant that the air passed over the asbestos before entering the saloons. The Derby Lightweights and 79xxx series Swindon cars additionally had a layer of asbestos sprayed on the underside of the floor, before the underframe equipment was fitted. Some types, particularly later sets, used glass-fibre insulation, but also had a layer of white asbestos in the floor as a barrier against underfloor fires.

It was the early 1980s before there was any new stock built to replace the first-generation sets. It was not a mass-building campaign like in the Fifties — the changeover period was very protracted. This resulted in another refurbishment scheme starting in 1992, branded 'facelifting', and was again aimed at vehicles that had the longest life expectancy. The replacement process was effectively complete by December 2003, when the last Met-Camm vehicles were withdrawn from the Manchester area.

However, Chiltern Railways took a Class 121 single unit out of sandite use and gave it an extensive overhaul, the interior being brought up to the standard of its new stock. This was to cover the Aylesbury–Princes Risborough line, freeing a modern set to allow a programme of overhauls to be undertaken. As I write this, another Class 121 has just been refurbished for Arriva Trains Wales, which will double the amount of first-generation vehicles in passenger use on the national network, 52 years after they were first introduced!

Little reference has been made in the captions to the shades of green depicted, and instead I have chosen to summarise the livery situation here. The images in the book do not always show the true shade and there were indeed variations between the paints used by different builders.

In the planning stages, DMUs were considered coaching stock and were destined to be painted carmine and cream, but it was then decided they were 'motive power', so the first sets emerged in 'Locomotive Green', with the lion-on-wheel logo used as per locomotives. As numbers grew it was then thought they should have their own livery, so in 1956 the policy was changed for all new cars and repaints to appear in a lighter shade, 'Multiple-unit' (or 'Stock') green, with the round coaching crest. The paint colours were standardised in 1960, changing back again to 'Locomotive Green', but retaining the coaching crest.

Early cars did not have whiskers or red bufferbeams, and these were added after concerns about how quiet these new trains were in approaching. The whiskers were replaced in 1963 by yellow panels on the lower half of the cab. Sometimes these were added by depots rather than during a full works repaint, and the ends of the whiskers could still be seen as they were wider than the yellow panel!

The introduction of Rail blue saw some variations in the amount of yellow used until it was standardised to cover the whole of the cab front. Plain blue was used for suburban and low-density stock while Inter-City and Cross-Country stock was painted blue/grey (as per Inter-City hauled stock). Refurbished cars were given their own livery of white with a blue band, until this proved impossible to maintain in a presentable form, so refurbished cars received blue/grey, and in time, plain blue was dispensed with in favour of blue/grey. There were several one-off liveries, but the next major changes were the introduction of an orange/black Strathclyde PTE livery in 1984, Network SouthEast (NSE) in 1989, and Regional Railways in 1992, which all come within the scope of this book.

The tables for each type show the vehicle numbers, with the regional prefix for where they were built (unfortunately there is no ER 'E'/NER 'NE' breakdown). The vehicle type is shown, and the number of seats, with the number of first-class seats first, if a composite vehicle. The formation for which the vehicle was built is shown if relevant, the weights are mainly from the BR diagram book (although some are from more reliable sources), and also quoted are the original BR diagram number, lot number and the year the first vehicle in that number range was delivered. The vehicle codes used are the later type: D = driving, M = motor, B = brake or buffet, F = first class, S = second class, C = composite, T = trailer.

DERBY LIGHTWEIGHTS
Built by British Railways, Derby Works

Above: After the first build of Lightweights, the hydraulic sets for the West Riding, Derby built the sets for the 'West Cumberland' scheme using 150hp engines and a four-speed gearbox, the first use of the drive train which became standard for a large percentage of DMUs to follow. They were introduced in three stages: Carlisle to Silloth on 29 November 1954; the Workington, Cockermouth, Keswick & Penrith line on 3 January 1955; Carlisle–Maryport–Workington–Whitehaven on 7 February 1955.

There were other differences in the first few batches of Lightweight vehicles. The West Riding and West Cumberland batches (Nos E79000-79020, E79500-79507, E79600-79612) had full-height windscreens, but problems with these meant that an internal strengthening bar was soon fitted

and all subsequent vehicles had each screen split into two. The windscreen wiper for a full screen was side mounted; on split screens this was on the divider with a blade top and bottom. The West Cumberland driver trailer cars also carried the lion-over-wheel emblem, but in general only power cars would normally carry these. Window bars were fitted to the passenger door droplights and in between the sliding lights, because of limited clearance on the Maryport & Carlisle line. The batch was delivered without whiskers, but by the time this view was taken on 15 June 1957 at Keswick, they had been added, along with a red bufferbeam (which was originally black). This was done to assist the visibility of approaching units. The red lens fitted over the marker light was an alternative to a tail light.
J. M. Chamney/Colour-Rail

Below: In the push to cut operating costs on branch lines, there were cases where passenger numbers did not justify a two-car DMU set, and so two 'double-ender' single cars were created for experiments on the Buckingham–Banbury line. The withdrawal of passenger services had been looming over the 16 3/4-mile branch, so to give the trial a fair chance, two new, unmanned halts were opened, at Radclive and Water Stratford. However, despite passenger receipts rising by 400-500% and operating costs falling by a third, the branch was still considered to be making an unacceptable loss and was scheduled for closure on 2 January 1960. It was given a last-minute reprieve, however, the closure being postponed until an alternative bus service could be provided, and the vehicles worked their last day on 31 December 1960.

The two vehicles are seen at Buckingham 10 days before closure, with No M79901 on the left and M79900, which had failed, on the right. The cab at the van end was quite cluttered, with all the items normally hidden at the rear end of a power car on display. The pipes near the cab corners were to fill the radiator header tanks which were originally located above the vestibules on Derby Lightweight cars. The two vehicles differed in the size of the luggage compartment. No M79900 had a smaller van, and subsequently an extra seating bay between the van and rear vestibule, resulting in a regular window there. On the other car, the van went right to the vestibule, represented by a smaller-width window. It was soon found that the van on the first vehicle was too small, so it was returned to Derby to have it enlarged, but it retained its full-size window.
T. Tice/Colour-Rail

Numbers	Type	Seats	Formation	Weight	Diagram	Lot No.	Year
E79000-79007	DMBS	61	Power twin	26 tons	501	30084	1954
M79008-79020	DMBS	61	Power twin	27 tons	503	30123	1954
E79021-79033	DMBS	56	Power/trailer	27 tons	504	30126	1955
E79034-79046	DMBS	56	Power/trailer	27 tons	504	30177	1955
M79118-79126	DMBS	52	Power/trailer	27 tons	633	30235	1955
M79127-79136	DMBS	52	Power/trailer	27 tons	633	30240	1956
E79137-79140	DMBS	52	Power/trailer	27 tons	527	30240	1956
M79141-79142	DMBS	52	Power/trailer	27 tons	633	30246	1956
M79143-79149	DMBS	52	Power/trailer	27 tons	633	30201	1956
E79150-79154	DMS	64	4-car	27 tons	518	30193	1955
M79169-79181	DMBS	52	Power/trailer	27 tons	633	30321	1956
M79184-79188	DMBS	52	Power twin	27 tons	633	30324	1956
M79189-79193	DMCL	9/53	Power twin	27 tons	510	30325	1956
E79250-79262	DTCL	16/53	Power/trailer	21 tons	505	30128	1955
E79325-79329	TBSL	45	4-car	21 tons	508	30194	1955
E79400-79404	TSL	61	4-car	21 tons	517	30195	1955
E79500-79507	DMCL	16/53	Power twin	27 tons	507	30085	1954
E79508-79512	DMC	20/36	4-car	27 tons	502	30192	1955
M79600-79612	DTCL	9/53	Power/trailer	21 tons	509	30124	1954
E79613-79625	DTCL	16/53	Power/trailer	21 tons	505	30127	1955
M79633-79635	DTCL	9/53	Power/trailer	21 tons	509	30325	1955
M79639-79647	DTCL	9/53	Power/trailer	21 tons	509	30236	1955
M79648-79657	DTCL	9/53	Power/trailer	21 tons	509	30241	1956
E79658-79661	DTCL	12/53	Power/trailer	21 tons	631	30241	1956
M79662	DTCL	12/53	Power/trailer	21 tons	642	30247	1956
M79663-79669	DTCL	12/53	Power/trailer	21 tons	642	30202	1956
M79670-79684	DTCL	12/53	Power/trailer	21 tons	511	30322	1956
M79900	DMBS	61	Single	27 tons	514	30380	1956
M79901	DMBS	52	Single	27 tons	515	30387	1956

Left: After the Banbury branch closed, these two vehicles took over the Bletchley–Buckingham service from the steam push/pulls, sometimes working with another vehicle attached. In this view, No M79901 has been through works since closure of the Banbury branch, the header tanks now being incorporated in the radiator, calling for the removal of the filler pipes on the cab, although the roof pipes were left on. Dummy jumper sockets are now fitted, along with jumper cables which are permanently in place, rather than stored in the cab. The vehicle also carries the coaching crest in place of the lion-over-wheel emblem. This car was withdrawn from Bletchley in December 1966, at just 10 years and four months old.
D. A. Hope/Colour-Rail

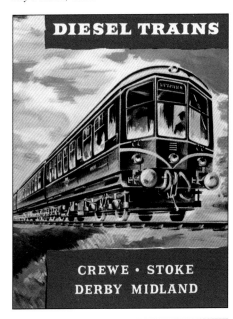

Above: The first sets built, the West Riding hydraulics, were withdrawn just before their 10th birthday. Their Leyland O600 125hp engines, Lysholm Smith torque converters and different control system, earned them this early demise and their own red triangle coupling code. They were the first DMUs introduced in this country, on 14 June 1954, between Leeds and Bradford. It was a fast service with severe gradients and so both vehicles in each set were powered. They could be easily identified by the triangular junction box for the jumper sockets just below the driver's window, there being no lower centre marker light and, like the West Cumberland units, they had side-mounted windscreen wipers. The eight sets were withdrawn in February 1964 and all sent to A. King's at Norwich for disposal, apart from this car, No E79500, which went to King's yard at Wymondham. It is seen being towed by an English Electric Type 1 through Rotherham on 6 May 1965. *Geoff Warnes/Colour-Rail*

Above: The introduction of Rail blue brought a couple of very short-lived variations when it appears that BR could not decide on how much yellow to use. There was either a small yellow panel, or the yellow covered the cab and the cab doors before it was decided to have just the cab front yellow. The small yellow panel type came in two sizes, either identical to that as carried with the previous green livery, or a larger variation which covered the whole bottom half of the cab front. The small panel was accompanied by double arrows on the driver's door and three-inch vehicle numbers rather than four-inch. One of these blue cars is paired with a green car in a train at Hunstanton, on a Bishops Stortford working in June 1967. The grille under the centre window has been removed and plated over. *Colour-Rail*

Below: Displaying a yellow diamond on a yellow cab has been achieved here by painting it on a black square. It is perhaps surprising that sets appeared in blue at all, being planned for an early withdrawal, with the last going in 1969. The other lines on which these sets had worked included: Lincolnshire, between Lincoln, Cleethorpes, New Holland, Skegness and Boston; East Anglia, Norwich to Dereham and Wells, Ipswich, Yarmouth, Cromer, Sheringham and Holt, Lowestoft and Dereham to King's Lynn; from Newcastle to Middlesbrough, Carlisle and York; from Birmingham to Sutton Coldfield and Lichfield; North Wales between Blaenau Ffestiniog and Llandudno, Bangor and Amlwch. Stratford sets worked the Romford to Upminster and Wickford to Southminster services, while there were also short spells in the Edinburgh area and South Wales. *Colour-Rail*

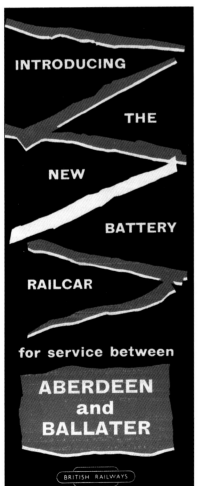

Above: Not in fact a DMU, but included here as the vehicles used Derby Lightweight bodyshells. The North of Scotland Hydro-Electric Board persuaded the BTC to try a battery railcar and offered a cheap electricity rate for the trial. Cowlairs kitted out a set with two traction motors and the 216 battery cells needed to power them, the vehicles being Nos Sc79998 and Sc79999. It entered service on the 43-mile Aberdeen–Ballater line on 21 April 1958. There were charging plants at both ends of the line, with 150 miles attainable between charges. Initially it was successful, but problems became more common and it started to spend periods out of use. A new type of battery fitted in June 1962 did little to help. The line closed in 1966 and the set was withdrawn, but was claimed for departmental use and it is now preserved for eventual use on the Royal Deeside Railway. It is seen here in Inverurie Works on 21 April 1962 in the company of 'J37' class 0-6-0 No 64579. It is easily identifiable by the lack of jumper sockets and no centre grille under the cab windows. *Colour-Rail*

Above: A further three Derby Lightweight vehicles went into departmental use, long enough to enter the preservation era. A former West Cumberland twin set became the Ultrasonic Test Train, and a single car became 'Test Coach Iris'. One of the latter's many uses was testing the North of Scotland RETB system on lines north of Inverness. It is seen in the TMD there, in the company of Class 37 No 37260, which has wires passing from it into the Test Coach. *Author*

MET-CAMM LIGHTWEIGHTS
Built by Metropolitan-Cammell

Numbers	Type	Seating	Weight	Diagram	Lot No
E79047-79075	DMBS	56	31½ tons	591	30190
M79076-79082	DMBS	52	31½ tons	592	30190
E79263-79291	DTSL	72	25 tons	593	30191
M79626-79632	DTCL	12/53	25 tons	594	30191

Above: British Railways soon realised that its own workshops could not build vehicles fast enough for its needs, so an order for vehicles was put out to tender. The lowest price came from Metropolitan-Cammell, but in time, all the companies involved received orders as the Modernisation Plan got underway. Subsequent orders meant that Met-Camm built 760 vehicles at Saltley before production of these vehicles ended. Ordered at the time the Derby Lightweights were being built, this first batch delivered in 1955 had compatible control equipment, identifiable by the waist-height jumper sockets. They also differed by having cowling below the bufferbeam, covering the front of the bogie. Poered by 150hp AEC engines, seven sets were for the Bury–Bacup line, numerically higher but delivered first, and comprised a DMBS and a DTC. The lower-numbered 29 sets were for East Anglia, and without first class they were formed DMBS + DTS. Here, two such sets are seen at Doncaster. There is a Met-Camm emblem affixed to one of the side windows, and it appears to have white lenses slotted in the front of the lower centre as well as non-driving side marker lights. The jumper socket lids have numbers marked on them to ensure they are coupled in the correct sequence! *Colour-Rail*

DIESEL PASSENGER TRAINS

Above right: When the vehicles passed through works they were repainted with lining that matched other vehicles, rather than Met-Camm's original three thin lines. With whiskers also now added, No E79270 leads a set out of King's Lynn for Dereham. The Eastern Region cars were used throughout East Anglia, but they also spent short spells in Scotland and at Lincoln as well as working from Stratford on services such as Romford–Upminster. *Colour-Rail*

Right: The ER sets had a slightly smaller guard's van, allowing an extra row of seats. There was no external difference other than one of the two small rear windows was not frosted. The DTS is now fitted with a rubber panel behind the driver's door in this view at Melton Constable on 7 March 1964. Some cars did make it into the blue livery before they were withdrawn, by 1969. Two DMBSs went into departmental use, allocated to Derby Technical Centre. None survives. *Colour-Rail*

CLASS 100
Built by Gloucester Railway Carriage & Wagon

Above: GRCW built two consecutive batches of power/trailer sets in 1957, later classed under TOPS as 100 with 150hp AEC engines. Each batch of 20 sets could be identified by a single top marker light (first) or two lower lamps (second). Eleven of the first batch were for the Manchester and Birmingham areas, with the remaining sets destined for Scotland for use on Edinburgh suburban services and the line to Glasgow Central via Shotts. Here, one of the second-batch sets arrives at Murrayfield, on the Princes Street–Leith North line, on 17 March 1962. The body colour continues on to the solebar. Some classes had 'LW' marked on the blue square to signify their lightweight underframe construction (with implications for tail loads), but these were identified by a 'G' instead. The first Scottish Region cars spent some time on loan to the LMR at Longsight and Llandudno, until it had a sufficient number of its own vehicles. *K. M. Falconer/Colour-Rail*

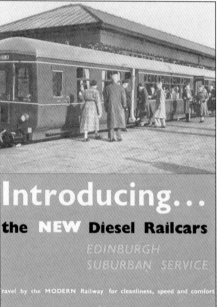

Numbers	Type	Class	Seating	Weight	Diagram	Lot No
Sc50339-50347	DMBS	100	52 2nd	30 tons 5cwt	536	30278
M50348-50358	DMBS	100	52 2nd	30 tons 5cwt	536	30278
Sc51108-51127	DMBS	100	52 2nd	30 tons 5cwt	536	30444
Sc56094-56102	DTC	143	12 1st, 54 2nd	25 tons	537	30279
M56103-56113	DTC	143	12 1st, 54 2nd	25 tons	537	30279
56300-56319	DTC	143	12 1st, 54 2nd	25 tons	537	30445

Above: There is an abundance of GRCW sets in this view of Dunfermline Lower on 22 October 1966. Now in the darker locomotive green with yellow panels, all three sets also display a livery difference peculiar to Scotland in the late green era — a band at cantrail height denoting first class saloons, which appears to be cream. Whiskers were rarely seen on the Gloucester twins as they seemed to jump straight to yellow panels. The closure of Edinburgh suburban lines meant that the class was spread throughout a greater area of Scotland, and the late 1960s saw sets move south to East Anglia to replace yellow diamond sets. Some also worked in the Newcastle area in 1967, covering for the South Tyneside electrics. *G. M. Staddon/Colour-Rail*

Above: The blue era saw small yellow panel and yellow cab door variations appear before settling on the normal yellow end. The passenger seats in the saloons can be seen, and appear to still have their original coverings. The whole vehicle is now non-smoking, with circle transfers on the windows having replaced the triangles. This class was not to be refurbished and withdrawals started in 1972, at first concentrating on the DTCs, leaving the DMBSs to be formed into hybrid sets. No M50342 is seen with a Class 104 vehicle at Newton Heath in 1977. *Ian Francis*

Above: Set No 73 is formed of a Class 100 DMBS and a Class 105 DTC, and is seen departing from Spalding. The power car has lost its two-digit route indicator box and has a patch on the roof above the cab, perhaps a repair to a dent. The note written above the closest blue square is the tail load limit. The ER lost its allocation by 1980, the vehicles either being withdrawn or moved to the LMR. One vehicle, No 53355, outlasted the rest, running as a power twin with the last '105', No 53812, finally going in 1988. The pair had been cleaned of asbestos as an assessment for carrying out this work on other members of their classes, but this did not go any further. *Colour-Rail*

Above: Eight Class 100 vehicles went into departmental use in a variety of roles, including a vehicle for weed-killing trains. Perhaps the most notable was a pair that became the ER General Manager's saloon. Branded the 'Stourton Saloon' it initially ran in blue before passing through Ilford in 1985 and emerging in a Provincial blue livery. Nos 975637 and 975664 were formerly Nos 56300 and 51122, and this view shows the inner end and an exhaust arrangement that could also be found originally on some other private builds such as Met-Camms and BRCW Class 104 sets. There is a cover, perhaps to protect the silencer from rain? The bodyside colours continued round the front of the vehicles, but with the dark blue band changing to yellow and a red buffer beam the livery made the vehicles look very dated. Four vehicles survive in preservation; one DMBS and three DTCs. *Malcolm Clements*

CLASS 101
Built by Metropolitan-Cammell

Above: Met-Camm units were allocated far more widely than any other type of DMU. Including the 79xxx and Rolls-Royce vehicles, 760 cars were built; 465 were for the ER and NER, 159 for the ScR and 136 for the LMR. They later spread to the Western Region where they gained access into Southern Region territory. Part of the Scottish order was 30 power/trailer Class 101 sets, all delivered to Dundee in May–July 1958, for use on local services, but they also saw more widespread operation. Here, a young admirer watches one of these units at Elie, on the Fife coast, on 22 July 1958. Despite the glistening paintwork it seems to be heavily stained on the top of the cab, and has possibly been stabled underneath somewhere where birds perch. Both vacuum pipes on the bufferbeam are white, and despite being brand new, the non-driver's side windscreen wiper has a wider sweep than required! *A. C. Renfrew/Colour-Rail*

Centre right: On vehicles delivered in the 'pre-whisker' era, these were often added at depots, resulting in some distinct variations. No E56074 has consistently thicker and straighter whiskers than is normal for a Met-Camm. By the time this photograph was taken, in 1962, the vehicle had spent a period on loan to Longsight (Manchester) away from its original allocation of Hull and was now allocated to South Gosforth (Newcastle). It is seen at West Wylam on a Haltwhistle service. *Colour-Rail*

Right: Now with yellow warning panels, this view at Haltwhistle on 14 May 1966 shows the original lining style on the left, with three narrow lines. The vehicles on the right have been turned out with just two bands, in the style of other DMUs. This does not seem to suit them as well, making them look fatter! *Colour-Rail*

Numbers	Type	Class	Seating	Weight	Lot No	Diagram	Formation	Year
E50138-50151	DMC(L)	101/1	12/45	32 tons	30249	BR 618	4-car	1956
E50152-50157	DMBS	101/2	52	32 tons	30252	BR 523	Power twin	1956/7
E50158-50163	DMC(L)	101/1	12/53	32 tons	30253	BR 620	Power twin	1956/7
E50164-50167	DMBS	101/2	52	32 tons	30254	BR 523	Power twin	1956/7
E50168-50171	DMC(L)	101/1	12/53	32 tons	30255	BR 620	Power twin	1956/7
E50172-50197	DMC(L)	101/1	12/53	32 tons	30256	BR 620	4-car	1957
E50198-50209	DMBS	101/2	52	32 tons	30259	BR 523	Power/trailer	1957
E50210-50233	DMBS	101/2	52	32 tons	30261	BR 523	Power/trailer	1957
E50234-50245	DMC(L)	101/1	12/45	32 tons	30263	BR 619	4-car	1957
E50246-50248	DMBS	101/2	52 or 44	32 tons	30339	BR 521 or BR 522	Power/trailer	1957
E50250-50259	DMBS	101/2	52	32 tons	30266	BR 523	Power twin	1957
E50260-50269	DMC(L)	101/1	12/53	32 tons	30267	BR 621	Power twin	1957
E50290-50292	DMBS	101/2	52	32 tons	30270	BR 523	3-car	1957
E50293-50296	DMBS	101/2	52	32 tons	30270	BR 523	Power/trailer	1957
M50303-50320	DMBS	101/2	52	32 tons	30275	BR 523	3-car	1958
M50321-50338	DMC(L)	101/1	12/53	32 tons	30276	BR 621	3-car	1958
E50745-50747	DMC(L)	101/1	12/53	32 tons	30271	BR 621	3-car	1957
E50748-50751	DMC(L)	101/1	12/53	32 tons	30271	BR 621	4-car	1957
M51174-51203	DMBS	101/1	52	32 tons	30467	BR 523	Power/trailer	1958
E51204-51223	DMBS	101/2	52	32 tons	30467	BR 523	Power/trailer	1958
Sc51224-51253	DMBS	101/2	52	32 tons	30467	BR 523	Power/trailer	1958
E51425-51434	DMBS	102/2	52	32 tons	30500	BR 523	Power twin	1959
E51435-51444	DMBS	102/2	52	32 tons	30500	BR 523	4-car	1959
Sc51445-51470	DMBS	102/2	52	32 tons	30500	BR 523	3-car	1959
E51495-51504	DMC(L)	102/1	12/53	32 tons	30501	BR 621	Power twin	1959
E51505-51514	DMC(L)	102/1	12/53	32 tons	30501	BR 621	4-car	1959
Sc51515-51540	DMC(L)	102/1	12/53	32 tons	30501	BR 621	3-car	1959
Sc51795-51801	DMBS	102/2	52	32 tons	30587	BR 523	3-car	1959
Sc51802-51808	DMC(L)	102/1	12/53	32 tons	30588	BR 621	3-car	1959
E56050-56061	DTC(L)	144	12/53	25 tons	30260	BR 630	Power/trailer	1957
E56062-56085	DTC(L)	144	12/53	25 tons	30262	BR 630	Power/trailer	1957
E56086-56089	DTC(L)	144	12/53	25 tons	30272	BR 630	Power/trailer	1957
E56218-56220	DTC(L)	144	12/45	25 tons	30340	BR 629	Power/trailer	1957
M56332-56361	DTC(L)	144	12/53	25 tons	30468	BR 630	Power/trailer	1957
E56362-56381	DTC(L)	144	12/53	25 tons	30468	BR 630	Power/trailer	1957
Sc56382-56411	DTC(L)	144	12/53	25 tons	30468	BR 630	Power/trailer	1957
E59042-59048	TS(L)	162	61	25 tons	30250	BR 622	4-car	1956
E59049-59055	TBS(L)	168	45	25 tons	30251	BR 626	4-car	1956
E59060-59072	TS(L)	162	71	25 tons	30257	BR 623	4-car	1957
E59073-59085	TBS(L)	168	53	25 tons	30258	BR 627	4-car	1957
E59086-59091	TS(L)	162	61	25 tons	30264	BR 622	4-car	1957
E59092-59097	TBS(L)	168	45	25 tons	30265	BR 626	4-car	1957
E59112-59113	TBS(L)	168	53	25 tons	30274	BR 627	4-car	1957
M59114-59131	TC(L)	171	12/53	25 tons	30277	BR 624	3-car	1958
E59302-59304	TS(L)	162	71	25 tons	30273	BR 623	3-car	1957
E59305-59306	TS(L)	162	71	25 tons	30273	BR 623	4-car	1957
E59523-59542	TC(L)	171	12/53	25 tons	30502	BR 624	4-car	1959
Sc59543-59568	TC(L)	171	12/53	25 tons	30502	BR 624	3-car	1959
Sc59686-59692	TC(L)	171	12/53	25 tons	30589	BR 624	3-car	1959
E59569-59572	TS(L)	164	71	25 tons	30510	BR 623		1960
E59573-59578	TSB(L)	165	53	25 tons	30511	BR 625		1960

Above: Thirteen four-car sets (DMC/TBS/TS/DMC) were delivered to Darlington for services to Saltburn. This batch was soon spread around though, often working as three-car sets with the TS removed. In this view, the leading DMC has the lining redone to match other DMU types. They were delivered in 1957, before the two-digit route indicator was introduced. *Colour-Rail*

Left: Seen at Haymarket on 14 August 1972, from the bridge that once carried the Caley line to Leith North, a three-car set formed as DMC/TBS/DMC, is seen heading for Kirkcaldy. Two Class 27 push-pull sets can be seen also on Glasgow–Edinburgh services and Haymarket station is in the distance. *G. M. Staddon*

Below left: A Class 101 set was chosen as a test-bed for the DMU refurbishment programme. With the age of vehicles approaching 20 years and no immediate sign of replacement, BR opted for a massive scheme to upgrade the DMU fleet. First, a prototype set was completed, passing through Doncaster Works in 1974, after which the set made a three-month tour of the country so that Passenger Transport Executives and other bodies with interests in local transport could inspect and comment on the design. Internally, the three vehicles were finished to different standards, and a new livery was applied, also with two options. On the side visible in this view at Glen Douglas, the blue stripe was narrower, while on the other side, it had what became the standard 12in stripe. The front end has been tidied up, with a miniature four-character route indicator visible in the non-driver's side cab window. The set is seen on a Glasgow to Oban working on 22 August 1975. *G. M. Staddon*

Above: A four-car refurbished set is seen at York. The short gutter sections that originally only covered the doors are apparent, but these were soon replaced with a full-length version. There is an additional silencer fitted vertically at the engine originally powered by either 150hp Leyland or AEC engines, the AECs were replaced by Leylands. Vehicle ends are blue and four marker lights are still carried. Normally the front end was cleaned up leaving just two. *Colour-Rail*

Above: The 1970s saw the introduction of local brandings on sets, at first representing sponsoring PTEs, but in time this was expanded to others such as 'Trans-Clyde', 'ScotRail' and, as seen on this set, 'MetroTrain', although Norwich is some way from the MetroTrain area! Ready to work a service to Sheringham, the number in the non-driver's side cab window of No E53202 identifies it as set No 70. When blue/grey was introduced there were inconsistencies in how low the grey went on the bodyside. *Colour-Rail*

Right: Set No 101310's blue/grey livery is enhanced by the cab window area being painted black. It is seen leaving Edinburgh Waverley in July 1986. *Colour-Rail*

Above: Tyseley went a bit further with the black on set No TS417, wrapping it round to meet the door. With 'WM' markings, it waits at Shrewsbury beside set No C803 which has an off-set headlight fitted. *Colour-Rail*

Below: The Strathclyde livery started to appear on DMUs from 1984, being applied to Classes 101 and 107. The Strathclyde Transport logo is in the centre of the vehicles and the BR logo on the cabs. Later variations saw the BR logo replaced with the SPT three-colour 'whoosh' emblem. No 101304 is at Glasgow Queen Street on 5 May 1990. *Author*

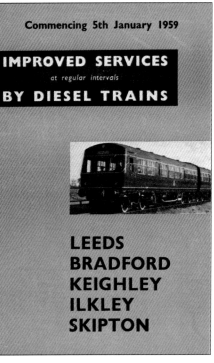

Commencing 5th January 1959

IMPROVED SERVICES
at regular intervals
BY DIESEL TRAINS

**LEEDS
BRADFORD
KEIGHLEY
ILKLEY
SKIPTON**

Right In 1986, eight DMBS vehicles were selected for conversion to two-car parcels units, which involved the removal of most passenger seats. They remained in blue and grey but with 'Express Parcels' lettering on the lower bodysides. The Parcels Sector red/yellow bodyside stripe was soon added. All were initially based at Neville Hill but later moved to Cambridge and were all withdrawn by July 1989. No 53218 (with No 53230) is seen at Leeds on 14 March 1988. *Malcolm Clements*

Centre right: A DTC appeared as an observation car in 1987 for use on trains from Inverness to Kyle of Lochalsh. It was fitted with ETH, most of the desk controls were taken out, the driver's partition greatly reduced, and seating altered. Initially, only the cab front was repainted, all in blue and embellished with Inverness depot's stag logo, but the vehicle was later repainted into a light green and cream livery and numbered 6300. Still carrying its original number, M54356, it is seen in Inverness station on 12 August 1987, with a mismatched door. Class 101s and 105s had the same body profiles as Mk1 coaches. *Author's collection*

Below: Many Met-Camm vehicles saw further non-passenger use, mainly as Sandite and route-learning cars. In 1987, a new Ultrasonic Test Train was built at Cardiff Cathays Works using two DMBS vehicles (Nos 53167 and 51433) with ex-SR EMU car No 62483 in between. The new departmental running numbers were 977392, 999602 and 977391 (set No 960001). The modifications were so extreme that it was barely recognisable as a former '101' set. It is seen stabled at Chester on 2 February 1990. *Kevin Dowd*

Right: Some '101' sets were latterly in NSE livery, such as this pair seen near Didcot, working the 16.00 Reading–Didcot on April 1992. Other than the small cab logo, they are devoid of NSE markings, but carry a 'Thames' logo on the van. One car has the window frames painted in the bodyside colours, while the other either has them unpainted or painted silver. This was a common difference over the years, as some works had their own interpretations of how vehicles should be finished. *Colour-Rail*

Below: Many years after refurbishment, it was recognised that selected first-generation units would be needed in traffic for some time until replacement DMUs gradually became available. A programme of 'facelifting' started in 1991 to again improve the appearance of the units for the travelling public. Less drastic changes were made than at refurbishment, it being more of a cosmetic makeover. It also marked the appearance of Regional Railways livery on DMUs. Set No 101657 (Nos 53211 and 54085) is in ex-works condition at New Mills South Junction on the 14.07 Manchester Piccadilly to Sheffield on 18 October 1991. A number of these facelifted sets saw out the rest of the class, and indeed, outlasted all other first-generation DMUs in passenger use on the national network, other than a Class 121 reintroduced by Chiltern Railways. Two sets received celebrity liveries: No 101685 was repainted in green for use on the Blaenau Ffestiniog branch and, for the start of Motherwell–Cumbernauld line services, No 101692 was painted in a new blue livery. The remaining sets became concentrated at Longsight, and worked their final passenger duties in the last days of 2003. Many have entered preservation. *Kevin Dowd*

CLASS 103
Built by Park Royal

Numbers	Type	Class	Seating	Weight	Diagram	Lot No
M50395-50414	DMBS	103	52 2nd	33 tons 8cwt	635	30286
M56150-56169	DTCL	145	16 1st and 48 2nd	26 tons 7cwt	645	30287

Left: A brand-new set pictured at Crewe on 2 May 1958, comprising Nos M56163 and M50408. This set's first allocation was to 5B, Crewe South. Although branded as Park Royal sets, they were not built in their North London Works, but at the Crossley Motor Works in Stockport, part of the same ACV group, in 1958. There were 20 power/trailer sets, and the vehicles had an interior more reminiscent of buses than any other first-generation DMUs, with full-width chromed handles along the top of the seats. The exhaust pipe has been painted green. *Colour-Rail*

Below: With a yellow panel replacing the speed-whiskers, a Park Royal set rolls into Barnt Green in 1960. The early days were spent on services from Birmingham and Chester as well as on the Harrow–Belmont line. *Colour-Rail*

Left: Some of the 150hp AEC-powered sets moved down to the Western Region, one of which is seen at Churston heading for Kingswear, labelled as set No P200. *Colour-Rail*

Below: In their later days the sets will always be remembered for working along the North Wales coast. This DMBS has its two-digit headcode box plated over, smartening its appearance, and is seen departing from Prestatyn on 13 August 1977. Considered non-standard, they were never refurbished and the final withdrawal was in 1983. Some survive in preservation. *Ian Francis*

Right: Some vehicles saw further use, one as a Sandite car, another pair was partially converted to a viaduct inspection unit, and one set became the RTC's 'Laboratory Coach No 5', a track recording unit (pictured) numbered RDB975090 and RDB975089, formerly Nos 56162 and 50396. It was replaced by a Class 150 unit. *Malcolm Clements*

Numbers	Type	Class	Seats	Formation	Weight	Diagram	Lot No	Year
M50420-50423	DMBS	104/2	52	3-car	31 tons	556	30290	1957
M50424-50427	DMCL	104/1	12/54	3-car	31 tons	558	30291	1957
M50428-50479	DMBS	104/2	52	3-car	31 tons	556	30293	1957
M50480-50531	DMCL	104/1	12/54	3-car	31 tons	558	30294	1957
M50532-50541	DMBS	104/2	52	Power/trailer	31 tons	556	30296	1958
E50542-50562	DMCL	104/1	12/51	4-car	31 tons	580	30298	1958
E50563-50583	DMCL	104/1	12/51	4-car	31 tons	559	30298	1958
E50584-50588	DMCL	104/1	12/51	4-car	31 tons	580	30301	1958
E50589-50593	DMCL	104/1	12/51	4-car	31 tons	559	30301	1958
E50594-50598	DMBS	104/2	52	Power/trailer	31 tons	557	30404	1958
M56175-56184	DTCL	140	12/54	Power/trailer	24 tons 10cwt	585	30297	1958
E56185-56189	DTCL	140	12/51	Power/trailer	24 tons 10cwt	581	30405	1958
M59132-59135	TCL	169	12/51	3-car	24 tons	582	30292	1957
M59136-59187	TCL	169	12/51	3-car	24 tons	582	30295	1957
E59188-59208	TSL	160	69	4-car	24 tons	583	30299	1958
E59209-59229	TBSL	166	51	4-car	25 tons	584	30300	1958
E59230-59234	TSL	160	69	4-car	24 tons	583	30302	1958
E59240-59244	TBSL	166	51	4-car	25 tons	584	30303	1958

Below left: The Birmingham Railway Carriage & Wagon Company built three types of DMUs for British Railways. These were 150hp Leyland engined which become Class 104, a more powerful version, later known as Class 110, and a batch of Derby-designed suburban sets (Class 118). There were 302 vehicles of the first type, formed into two, three or four-car sets for the NER and LMR. The lighter shade of green shows up well in this view of a power car and trailer set seen at Alston on 23 September 1961. *J. S. Davies/Colour-Rail*

Right: All vehicles were built with the two-digit route indicator, but there were variations in the marker lights. Nos 50420-50443 and 50480-50495 received just a top light, the remaining power cars having two lower lights. All the four-car sets were for the NER and one of these is seen at Garforth in September 1959 on a Hull–Leeds service. The whiskers are in a different colour from the lining, denoting that they had been added later. *D. A. Kelso/Colour-Rail*

Below: The single-lamp version is illustrated here: all these were originally part of LMR three-car sets. The interior of the vehicles differed between the regions, the LMR preferring wood-veneered wall panels while the NER opted for laminates. With a nice clean roof dome, a BRCW set is seen at Dove Holes on 28 March 1965 heading for Buxton. Of all the routes worked by the class, it was this one with which they became synonymous. *D. Cawthorn/Colour-Rail*

Right: At the start of the Rail blue era the Class 104s appeared in both the small panel and yellow cab door variations, the latter pictured here working a Railway Enthusiasts' Club railtour. *Colour-Rail*

Below right: In service, the '104s' worked over many routes on the BR network, covering most, if not all of the DMU diagrams of their home depots. Allocations included: Ayr, Bletchley, Buxton, Cambridge, Carlisle Kingmoor, Chester, Crewe North, Crewe South, Cricklewood, Darlington, Derby Etches Park, Eastfield, Hull Botanic Gardens, Hull Springfield, Leeds Neville Hill, Llandudno Junction, Longsight, Newton Heath, Norwich, Old Oak Common, Ryecroft, South Gosforth, Stoke, Stratford, Toton, Tyseley, York and Walsall Monument Lane. In the more conventional blue livery, a set is seen at Aylesbury in June 1978. *Colour-Rail*

Below: Thirteen three-car sets had their suspension modified and were dedicated to Manchester–Blackpool services. These were identified by the application of a white bodyside stripe, as shown on this DMC at Swindon Works. It has also had its two-digit headcode box plated over. Buxton was noted for embellishing its sets with white domes, red bufferbeams and latterly, black window surrounds. *Colour-Rail*

Above: One of the most unusual liveries to be carried by a DMU was on this set, which was soon branded the 'Mexican Bean'. Nos 53424 and 53434 (which had been part of the only three-car blue/grey '104' set) were transferred from Buxton to Eastfield and repainted to operate a mid-week additional Crianlarich–Oban service in the summer season. It was aimed at the tourist market and gave better connections between Oban and Fort William. Stabled at Oban, it regularly travelled to Glasgow on the back of a locomotive-hauled set for fuelling and servicing. It is seen at Tyndrum Lower on 24 June 1986. *J. Chalcraft/Colour-Rail*

Left: None of the class was refurbished, but some did appear in blue/grey livery, such as this centre car, No M59183, standing withdrawn at Chester, minus its seats, on 30 October 1989. The lack of roof vents shows that the vehicle had been stripped of asbestos. One notable set that ran in blue/grey was a power twin that had one engine removed from each car as an experiment in an attempt to cut back on maintenance costs. Nos 50446 and 50521 were renumbered 78851 and 78602 as part of set EXP DM352, which could easily be identified by a black stripe across the front of the cab. No further Class 104s were so converted, but Rolls-Royce-engined Met-Camms. *Robert Simpson*

Left: Some vehicles passed through Doncaster Works in 1988/89, emerging in NSE livery, a number being formed into power twins for Barking to Gospel Oak services, which they operated until replaced by '115s' and were then moved on to the Thames Line. Here, set No L263 stands at Slough ready to work the 13.20 to Windsor & Eton Central on 24 March 1992. Paired with DMBS No 53540 is Class 121 DTS No 54289. This was the final Class 104 vehicle to remain in traffic, being withdrawn in October 1993. Thirteen of these vehicles are now preserved. *Kevin Dowd*

Numbers	Type	Class	Seats	Formation	Weight	Diagram	Lot No	Year
E50249	DMBS	105/2	52		30 tons 10cwt	548	30505	1959
E50359-50372	DMBS	106/2	52	Power/trailer	29 tons	525	30280	1956
E50373-50389	DMBS	105/2	52	Power/trailer	29 tons	525	30282	1957
M50390-50394	DMBS	105/2	52	Power/trailer	29 tons	525	30284	1957
M50752-50770	DMBS	105/2	52	3-car	30 tons	528	30352	1957
M50771-50784	DMBS	105/2	52	Power twin	30 tons	528	30352	1957
M50785-507803	DMCL	105/1	12/51	3-car	30 tons	529	30353	1957
M50804-50817	DMCL	105/1	12/51	Power twin	30 tons	529	30353	1957
E51254-51301	DMBS	105/2	52	Power/trailer	30 tons	532	30469	1958
E51471-51472	DMBS	105/2	52	Power/trailer	30 tons 10cwt	548	30503	1959
Sc51473-51494	DMBS	105/2	52	Power/trailer	30 tons 10cwt	548	30503	1959
E56114-56127	DTCL	141	12/51	Power/trailer	23 tons	526	30281	1956
E56128-56144	DTCL	141	12/51	Power/trailer	23 tons	526	30283	1957
M56145-56149	DTCL	141	12/51	Power/trailer	23 tons	526	30285	1957
E56412-56459	DTCL	141	12/51	Power/trailer	24 tons	533	30470	1958
E56460-56461	DTCL	141	12/51	Power/trailer	24 tons	549	30504	1959
Sc56462-56483	DTCL	141	12/51	Power/trailer	24 tons	549	30504	1959
M59307-59325	TSL	170	69	3-car	23 tons	530	30354	1957

Top left: A three-car set at Hathern on 13 May 1961 working a Nottingham Midland to Birmingham New Street service. There were two variations in the two-digit box: the LMR cars had a one-piece glass version (as here) and the ER and ScR had two pieces of glass. The Cravens front was normally made more attractive by the unpainted aluminium window frames, but despite still not having whiskers added, this set has had its frames painted. They had 150hp engines from Leyland (106s) or AEC (105s). *Colour-Rail*

Top: The ER batch numbered E51254–51301 (DMBSs) and E56412–56459 (DTCs) were delivered to Lincoln and Cambridge, but within a few months some of these sets were moved to Hornsey to take over King's Cross suburban services on the Great Northen line. This pair, led by No E56416, is seen at Hatfield on 5 September 1960. The class also had differences in the layout of the guard's van, some such as this set having the van doors nearer the front with a small window between them and the rear while others had the doors right at the rear. *Colour-Rail*

Above: Scottish Region cars were delivered to Kittybrewster, except the final one. They were introduced to the Buchan lines —between Aberdeen, Peterhead and Fraserburgh, and Fraserburgh and St Combs, in June 1959. They also worked the services to Ballater on the diagram opposite the battery multiple-unit. The final set was delivered to Hamilton in June 1959, where it was joined in the same month by Nos Sc51482–51493 (and trailers) transferred from Kittybrewster. Oban was not a normal destination for the class, but a pair is seen there, and the rear version of van doors can be seen on the power car. Seating in the DTC is maroon in second class and blue in first class. *A. C. Renfrew/Colour-Rail*

Above left: No M50770 is at the head of a three-car set at Nottingham Midland station in 1967. These sets were built as DMBS/TS/DMC and so the only first-class section was at the front of the DMC. Pressure from first-class passengers for an independent non-smoking section saw a saloon in some centre cars converted to suit this accommodation, making them TCs. *Colour-Rail*

Left: No E51282 has been fitted with the rubber panels to prevent single-line tablet damage behind the cab doors. This vehicle was allocated to Cambridge and would have run on local services there and between Manningtree and Dovecourt, and Witham and Maldon, amongst others. Sets were also known to work Cambridge–Birmingham services. In the early 1970s, a small number of the early ER power/trailer sets went to North West England to replace Carlisle's Derby Lightweights. *Colour-Rail*

Above: A train of two two-car Class 112 sets, with the leading vehicle in the blue with small yellow panel livery, calls at Walthamstow. Note the leading set is formed from two DMBs. This version has the smaller example of the yellow panel and looks more attractive. *Colour-Rail*

Below: The larger version of the yellow panel did not look as good! A mixed liveried set passes Potters Bar on 15 April 1967. *M. Burnett/Colour-Rail*

Top: In the changeover period between four marker lights and the two-digit box, there would be vehicles partially constructed to accommodate four lamps, before Cravens were instructed by the BTC to fit the two-digit box. So there are some vehicles in several classes that have the mounting for the top lamp, but do not have such a lamp! Showing its LMR version of the two-digit box with the single piece of glass is this two-car set at Lidlington in August 1975. In ex-works condition, it lacks a yellow stripe for first-class, but the orange curtains are certainly evident! The vehicles should be from the 56145–56149/50390–50394 range. *Colour-Rail*

Above: Another headcode variation is seen at Hull, the two lower lamps having been removed and plated over, leaving just a top light, in the same fashion as the Class 114s. In a similar manner, once the two-digit route code became obsolete some cars had the two lower marker lights removed, replaced by two white dots in the two-digit box. *Colour-Rail*

Above: The class was not refurbished as they were scheduled for early withdrawal. A few ScR cars made it into blue/grey, the rest remaining in blue until the end, other than one set repainted into green in April 1986. It contained vehicles Nos 53359 (the first built) and 54122. Because the vehicles had to have a yellow panel, speed whiskers were added in black. For a time it had a red band above the cab windows which extended up to the rainstrip and around the destination box, as it does here, when seen at Colchester. The final vehicles left passenger service in 1988. Three vehicles are in preservation. *Colour-Rail*

Below: Some vehicles saw use as route learner/Sandite cars while others became parcel cars. All of these remained in blue, some had the red/yellow stripe, others did not, and all had the 'Express Parcels' markings, some on top of the stripe, others below! They were all pairs of DMBSs, and Nos 53367 and 53369 are seen at York on 12 May 1987. The destination blind also states 'Express Parcels'. *Colour-Rail*

CLASS 107
Built by British Railways' Derby Works

Numbers	Type	Class	Seats	Weight	Diagram	Lot No
Sc51985-52010	DMBS	107/2	52	34 tons 10cwt	639	30611
Sc52011-52036	DMC(L)	107/1	12/53	35 tons	649	30612
Sc59782-59807	TS(L)	161	71	28 tons	647	30613

Above: The last sets that Derby C&W Works built were 26 triple sets for the Scottish Region in 1960/62, to a design which used elements from previous builds. They were low-density units, with a similar layout to the Class 108s, but were an all-steel construction. The bodyside profile matched Derby's other steel vehicles with a more angled lower side than the alloy cars. Face on, the cab was indistinguishable from the Class 115s except by the small, round buffers. AEC 150hp engines were fitted when new, replaced in the 1970s with Leylands. All were delivered new to Hamilton, but this fairly new set is seen with a Met-Camm unit at Dalmeny Junction on a down Dundee service in June 1961. *D. A. Kelso/Colour-Rail*

Above right: The sets being delivered quite late, whiskers did not last long, being replaced by yellow warning panels. In common with other Derby designs, the exhausts originally joined above the gangways and emitted through a single box, as more commonly seen on GRCW 'bubble' cars. Here, No Sc52004 is the rear car on another '101/107' formation, leaving Glasgow Central on the lines that head west. *D. A. Hope/Colour-Rail*

Right: The change to Rail blue saw the sets painted in plain blue, a few initially just having a small yellow panel before the full yellow end appeared. Largs was a popular Ayrshire seaside town, and this view on 2 September 1972 has seven sets present. *G. M. Staddon*

Top: The class was refurbished, but only in the era when blue/grey had replaced the white livery. Generally, the four-character route indicator was blanked over, but some '107s' survived with these longer than they should have done. Their main duties were local and interurban services along the central belt of southern Scotland, between Ayr and Edinburgh, and this set is seen on a Glasgow Central–Edinburgh working, leaving Slateford for the capital on 10 November 1984. They had carried set numbers for many years, originally in the ScR 1xx series, but from 1981, the six-digit, TOPS system was introduced, and they became Nos 107425 to 107449. Hybrid sets could see cars carrying set numbers from a different class, but as this one does not have any Class 101 vehicles it cannot be explained why it is numbered 101366! Originally branded 'GG Trans-Clyde', the 'GG' part has been removed, marking the change to the SPTE. Later on in the blue/grey era, the cab window surrounds were painted black. Over the years they were allocated to Hamilton (HM), Ayr (AY), Eastfield (ED) and Haymarket (HA). By 1982 the class was mainly based at Ayr shed. *G. M. Staddon*

Above: This orange livery, officially known as 'Strathclyde Red', was introduced on EMUs, then spread to Glasgow-based DMUs, the first being set No 107444 in 1984. It was soon applied to other Class 107s and Class 101s. This view shows a set in this livery, back at its birthplace of Derby on 13 September 1986. The closest car is from No 107446, but the end of the TS is branded set No 441. Note the sticks in the DMBC droplights, and it looks as if tables have been fitted in the centre saloon! In 1989, the remaining 20 sets were transferred to Eastfield and the set numbers revised to 107025 to 107049, although the fourth digits were soon changed to make them into the 7xx series. In July 1991, the sets were moved en masse again, from west to east, with Haymarket becoming their final home. After replacement on passenger duties, some vehicles went on to Sandite use, and eleven vehicles have been preserved. *G. W. Parry/Colour-Rail*

CLASS 108
Built by British Railways, Derby Works

Above: When Derby returned to building alloy vehicles in 1958, it used the original Derby Lightweight body, but with steel ends, in the style of its steel vehicles and the then-standard blue square code. They proved to be very successful vehicles in traffic, and production continued through to 1961 with 331 built. These two newly built sets are seen at Blaenau Ffestiniog North in April 1959. The handrail at the driver's door is connected to the gutter and passes through the stepboard. This was hollow, and acted as the drain pipe for the gutters, and was a common feature on many units. When the pipes kept blocking up, normal handrails were fitted and holes drilled in the underside of the gutters for the water to drain out at appropriate places. Leyland 150hp engines were used throughout the class, and the Derby design of common exhaust outlet above the gangway was also used from new. *Colour-Rail*

Above: Class 108s were not unknown in Scotland. Some were delivered new (on loan) to Leith Central and in the short period between the end of steam and electrification of the Gourock route (1966/67) a variety of units (including '108s') were drafted in from all over the country to cover services. The '108s' had been delivered in two, three and four-car formations, three-car sets being the least common with only five built for the ER. Here, a DMC and TS from one of these sets is seen entering Glasgow Central from Gourock, with a '101' DMBS at the rear. The SC prefix has been added to DMC No 50645, and it stands out as it is a different shade from the number. The vehicle has been garnished with the stripe for first-class. The class returned to Scotland, to the Edinburgh area in the mid-1980s, as arrival of new stock cascaded units about the network. *Colour-Rail*

Numbers	Type	Class	Seats	Formation	Weight	Diagram	Lot No
E50599-50619	DMBS	108/2	52	Power/trailer	29 tons	543	30406
E50620-50624	DMBS	108/2	52	3-car	29 tons	543	30406
M50625-50629	DMBS	108/2	52	Power/trailer	29 tons	543	30407
E50630-50641	DMC(L)	108/1	12/50	4-car	28 tons	544	30408
E50642-50646	DMC(L)	108/1	12/50	3-car	28 tons	544	30408
M50924-50935	DMBS	108/2	52	Power/twin	29 tons	543	30460
M50938-50987	DMBS	108/2	52	Power/trailer	29 tons	543	30465
M51416-51424	DMBS	108/2	52	Power/trailer	29 tons	634	30498
M51561-51572	DMC(L)	108/1	12/52	Power/twin	28 tons	609	30461
M51901-51921	DMBS	108/2	52	Power/trailer	29 tons	634	30601
M51922-51950	DMBS	108/2	52	Power/twin	29 tons	634	30601
M52037-52065	DMC(L)	108/1	12/53	Power/twin	28 tons	638	30660
E56190-56210	DTC(L)	142	12/53	Power/trailer	21 tons	640	30409
M56211-56215	DTC(L)	142	12/53	Power/trailer	21 tons	640	30410
M56221-56270	DTC(L)	142	12/53	Power/trailer	21 tons	640	30466
M56271-56279	DTC(L)	142	12/53	Power/trailer	22 tons	646	30499
M56484-56504	DTC(L)	142	12/53	Power/trailer	22 tons	646	30602
E59245-59250	TBS(L)	167	50	4-car	23 tons	546	30412
E59380-59385	TS(L)	161	68	4-car	22 tons	547	30411
E59386-59390	TS(L)	161	68	3-car	23 tons	545	30493

The class received both the small yellow panel and yellow cab door variations in the early days of blue, the latter being seen on this two-car set at Weekday Cross in October 1967. The unit is heading away from the camera, carrying a tail lamp as the use of red bulbs in the marker lights, to replace tail lamps, was still a few years away. Vehicles with toilets had a small expansion tank fitted on the roof.
Colour-Rail

Top: Once the original Derby Lightweights were eliminated from West Cumberland, these later Derby Lightweights took over, and were fitted with window bars. This pair of power/trailer sets is seen at Threlkeld, working the 11.05 Keswick–Penrith on 29 February 1972. *Colour-Rail*

Above: Built without asbestos insulation, the '108s' were an ideal candidate for refurbishment, and a set is seen on display at York in September 1975 after this treatment. The white/blue stripe livery included a brown underframe and also notable is the WYPTE logo. There is now a mini four-character route indicator in the non-driving side cab window, the now-obsolete original two-character version being neatly plated over. *Colour-Rail*

Above: The NER received the first builds of the '108s' in 1958, in two, three and four-car formations, for use on routes such as Scarborough–Whitby and Whitby–Middlesbrough. The remainder of the class, all two-car sets, went to the LMR. Here, a four-car set is seen in one of the centre roads at York on 2 August 1983. The refurbished livery has given way to blue/grey, including MetroTrain branding, and the brackets for the coach boards just below cantrail level have gone, smartening the appearance. The use of the marker lights as tail lights is now evident. *Colour-Rail*

Top right: In 1960, a change was made to the cab design. A four-character headcode was fitted to the dome; the destination display being relocated to the top of the central cab window and the two-character box eliminated. The last set constructed to the original pattern was Nos M50935 and M51572 and the first set to the new design was Nos M51416 and M56271. After the four-character code became redundant, this was covered over, as seen in this set at Newport in June 1992. No W52038 has by this time received black cab window surrounds, while aluminium chequer-plate has been used to combat frequent bashings from the bufferbeam air hose, which frequently freed itself from its dummy coupling when at speed. Another difference on later cars was the moving of the coolant filler from the bodyside to the solebar, which accompanied a move of the header tank from underneath seats in the saloons to being integral to the radiator itself. Comparing this with the earlier picture at Glasgow Central, the exhaust system layout has been modified from the previous arrangement. Vehicles working in the area also received the Valley Train branding. Another variation came from Buxton depot, which applied white cab roof domes to most of its allocation during the early 1980s — something of a tradition at that depot, its Class 104s being famed for this also. When Buxton depot lost its DMU allocation, the vehicles were dispersed, but the white domes generally remained during the late 1980s at depots such as Chester, Tyseley and Swansea (Landore). *Colour-Rail*

Right: Carlisle painted a set (Nos 53364 and 54247) back into green for an open day at Carlisle Currock in 1986, and it is seen at Barrow that September. Regulations meant keeping the yellow panel, so the whiskers were painted on top of this. Later, the yellow was extended the full height of the cab. The white drawbar hook would not have stayed that colour for long!

Unusually, the 'LW' was painted below the blue square and there also seems to be extensive lettering on the rear of the trailer car. There are many variations from the original green styling, such as the inner bufferbeams would have been black and the trailer cars did not carry crests — other than the original Lightweights that worked in the area that is! The class had variations in the brake pipe arrangements. All sets delivered to the ER had their pipes mounted on the bufferbeam, those delivered to the LMR (except for the first five sets), having these pipes mounted below the bufferbeam, as pictured. *Colour-Rail*

Right: The final livery carried by the '108s' was NSE, and in the late 1980s some were formed into hybrid sets — a Class 108 DTC with a Class 115 DMBS. Such a pair is seen at Watford South Junction on Saturday, 21 July 1990. This shows clearly the difference between high and low-density cars, and the different lengths of the cars is also notable. The last of the class were withdrawn in 1993 and many have entered preservation. *Mel Holley*

CLASS 109
Built by Wickham

Numbers	Type	Class	Seating	Weight	Diagram	Lot No
E50415-50419	DMBS	109	59	27 tons	606	30288
E56170-56174	DTCL	146	16/ 50	22? tons	607	30289

Above: In this country, Wickham of Ware was better known for building its permanent way trolleys, but it had been building railcars for export for many years and fought to be allowed to build passenger vehicles for the home market. It was given an order for five 150hp Leyland-engined power/trailer sets, which were built using a distinctly different method of construction than any other units of the time. The body framework was built up with square-section steel tubes forming a stress-bearing box girder that did not need a conventional underframe. They were then clad in aluminium panelling. The first set entered traffic in the autumn of 1957 and perhaps it was fortunate that Wickham was not given a bigger order, as it took a further year until the last of the five sets was delivered. The first sets were delivered without whiskers, as in this view of Nos E56171 and E50416 at Fambridge. *Colour-Rail*

Above: The last set is thought to have been delivered with whiskers and the others soon had them applied. The 12.57 Norwich–Colchester is seen after arrival at its destination on 6 August 1960. The Wickham units worked solely on the ER, mainly on branch lines and local services in East Anglia, and the writing was on the wall for many of these lines not long after they were delivered. This allowed Wickham to buy back two sets in 1961, which were then exported to Trinidad and Tobago. The railway there closed in 1968. Some parts of these vehicles survived after services ended there, in use as dwellings and road-side cafes! *Colour-Rail*

Above: The number of sets in BR service dropped to two in 1967 when one became the ER General Manager's saloon. The remaining sets were painted into blue soon after, as in this view of a DMBS unusually working as a hybrid with a Cravens DTC. It is heading for Sudbury out of Chappel & Wakes Colne station, which nowadays also hosts the East Anglian Railway Museum, as well as being served by trains of the 'one' franchise. In addition to the unusual body construction, the interior was also notable for its distinctive design, with its art-deco style draught screens and a suspended ceiling channel. *Colour-Rail*

Below: The '109s' were withdrawn from passenger service in 1971, but the ER General Manager's saloon continued in use for some time after that. It had gone through an extensive refurbishment, revamping the interiors and adding kitchen facilities where the guard's van had been. This meant changes to window arrangements, doors being plated over, and the straightening of the gutter alignment at the front. A distinctive feature was the aluminium double arrows, as used on EMUs being built at the time. Painted into Rail blue, it had small yellow panels for a very short spell before gaining full yellow ends, as in this view at King's Cross in October 1977. It continued in this use until 1980, after which it entered preservation and was in the limelight when it became the first DMU to receive a Heritage Lottery Grant and underwent a high-profile restoration back to its original condition. *Colour-Rail*

CLASS 110
Built by Birmingham Railway Carriage & Wagon

Numbers	Type	Class	Seating	Weight	Diagram	Lot No
E51809-51828	DMBC	110/1	12/33	32 tons	564	30592
E51829-51848	DMCL	110/2	12/54	31 tons 10cwt	563	30593
M52066-52075	DMBC	110/1	12/33	32 tons	564	30691
M52076-52085	DMCL	110/2	12/54	31 tons 10cwt	563	30692
E59693-59712	TSL	163	72	24 tons	648	30594
M59808-59817	TSL	163	72	24 tons	648	30693

Above left: The final private-build of first-generation unit was further BRCW sets, and these were basically an updated version of the Class 104s. The cab front was redesigned to incorporate the four-character box, the bodyside lights were fitted in alloy frames rather than flush with the body panels, and more powerful engines were fitted to suit the lines on which the were to run. The batches were built one after another, for the NER (20 sets) and LMR (10 sets), differing only on the interior finishings to meet the specifications of each region. Those for the LMR were for use on the former Lancashire & Yorkshire main line, which earned them the name of Calder Valley sets. The 180hp Rolls-Royce engines gave them a very high power/weight ratio, and the 'reversed' whiskers that joined the lining enhanced their appearance. They entered traffic on 1 January 1962, with duties mainly centring round the Sowerby Bridge–Manchester line. Destinations included Leeds Central, Bradford Exchange, Manchester Victoria, Liverpool Exchange, Blackpool Central, Southport Chapel Street, York, and Wakefield. *Colour-Rail*

Below left: The layout of underframe equipment caused maintenance problems and made them more liable to catch fire. By the time they were ten years old there had been 92 recorded fires, mainly due to the exhaust and heating systems, which took some time to rectify. In the mid 1970s several sets had an additional trailer from Class 104s for a short period, making them into four-car sets. This March 1979 view shows a '110' bound for Leeds, pre-refurbishment, but with the headcode out of use, and one engine on the rear car in need of some attention! Both types of power car featured first class, as the yellow stripes clearly demonstrate. *Colour-Rail*

Above: These being one of the newest builds, refurbishment came late in the programme. One DMC was not treated: this was an odd car due to its partner being lost through fire damage. The cost of refurbishing a spare vehicle could not be justified, so it was withdrawn. Three trailers did not get treated, as near the end of the programme it was decided that only ten three-car sets were required. These three cars were withdrawn as were 15 other trailers which had just been through Doncaster Works! Only the early refurbishments emerged in the white with blue stripe livery, the rest going to blue/grey, one of which is seen at Mirfield on 5 March 1983 containing power cars Nos 51847 and 52073. Final withdrawals were in March 1990 with one two-car and a three-car set surviving into preservation. *Colour-Rail*

NEW AND
IMPROVED
SERVICES BY

DIESEL TRAIN

HARROGATE LEEDS
BRADFORD
YORK WAKEFIELD
MANCHESTER
LIVERPOOL

Commencing
1st Jan 1962

Numbers	Type	Class	Seats	Formation	Weight	Diagram	Lot No	Year
M50134-50137	DMBS	111/2	52	Power/trailer	33 tons	BR 520	30248	1957
E50270-50279	DMC(L)	111/1	12/53	3-car	33 tons	BR 616	30268	1957
E50280-50289	DMBS	111/2	52	3-car	33 tons	BR 524	30338	1957
E51541-51550	DMBS	111/2	52	2/3-car	33 tons	BR 615	30508	1959/60
E51551-51560	DMC	111/1	12/53	2/3-car	33 tons	BR 617	30509	1959/60
M56090-56093	DTC(L)	147	12/53	Power/trailer	25 tons	BR 628	30337	1957
E59100-59109	TS(L)	164	71	3-car	25 tons	BR 623	30269	1957
E59569-59572	TS(L)	164	71	3-car	25 tons	BR 623	30510	1959/60
E59573-59578	TSBL	165	53	3-car	25 tons	BR 625	30615	1960

Above: Rolls-Royce 180hp engines were also used on some Met-Camm units. There were three batches, starting in 1957 with four power/trailer sets for the LMR's Manchester area. Later in the year, 10 three-cars were built for the NER at Bradford, and finally a further 10 three-car sets went to the NER in 1959. The Met-Camm buffet cars were ordered with the third batch and were considered to be '111s' but in reality ran more often in '101' sets. All three batches differed in front-end layout: the first had four lamps, the second two lamps and a two-digit box, and the third had two lower lamps and a four-digit headcode box. Being the only Met-Camms with this box made the third batch easy to identify; the first two can only be differentiated from '101s' by underframe details, such as the larger radiators. This view at Skipton was taken on 2 May 1970, and the Met-Camm is working the 11.50 Skipton–Carlisle on the last day of the service. *Colour-Rail*

Above right: This close-up view at Upminster shows how the four-character box spoiled the look of the Met-Camms. When these became obsolete they were neatly plated over, the destination box remaining in its lower position. Also notable are the small gutters, which were only fitted above doors. In common with the '101s', these were later replaced by full-length gutters. *Colour-Rail*

Right: After the success of an experiment conducted by Doncaster Works on Class 104s Nos 50446 and 50521 in 1982, it was decided to remove one engine and its associated equipment from each of the remaining 36 Class 111 power cars as a maintenance and cost-saving measure. Centre trailers were removed where necessary and redeployed in other units, the remaining cars being paired together as power twins. With just one engine per car they had a combined 360hp, half the normal power, but still more than a 150hp-engined power/trailer set. These units were operated by Neville Hill (NL) depot in Leeds, and carried MetroTrain and South Yorkshire PTE logos. Vehicles so treated remained in the blue and grey livery but were renumbered in the 78xxx series. This is Nos 78960 and 78710 at Barnsley on 15 June 1985. All Rolls-Royce-engined vehicles were withdrawn by 1989 with none being preserved, although three early vehicles did join the departmental fleet. *Geoff Warnes/Colour-Rail*

CLASS 112/113
Built by Cravens

Right: The only first-generation power cars built with single engines were 50 power twins built for the LMR in 1960. These Cravens sets all had 238hp Rolls-Royce engines, but half were built with gearboxes ('112s') and half with torque converters ('113s'). All were for the same duties, and this was claimed to be an experiment to compare mechanical and hydraulic transmission on an equal basis. The two types could easily be told apart, as the hydraulic cars had a four-character box, uniquely combined with the route indicator. The mechanical cars were difficult to distinguish from the 150hp vehicles, clues being a single exhaust port coming through the roof, the sides lacked fuel filling points having just a smaller coolant filler in the centre on the driver's side only, and the revised underframe layout. On the non-driving side the RR cars had the battery box at the rear rather than on the front, and there was no radiator. On the driver's side there was a distinctly bigger radiator, mounted further forward than the 150hp-engined cars. Here, two brand-new mechanical sets are seen passing through Dinting, led by No 51723. The black gutter and black marker lights are of note. Also, despite passing under electrified lines, there are no electrification warning flashes carried! *Colour-Rail*

Numbers	Type	Class	Seating	Weight	Diagram	Lot No
M51681-51705	DMBS	112/2	52	30 tons	602	30533
M51706-51730	DMCL	112/1	12/51	30 tons	603	30534
M51731-51755	DMBS	113/2	52	30 tons	604	30535
M51756-51780	DMCL	113/1	12/51	30 tons	605	30536

Left: The cars were built for services in the LMR Central Division and in the Liverpool–St Helens area, where the gradients on the former Lancashire & Yorkshire lines required more power. They were introduced as the last phase of the North East Lancashire diesel scheme and began working between Manchester, Accrington, Burnley, Colne and Skipton, and between Accrington and Preston, on 6 March 1961. Although generally associated with Accrington, they were also allocated to other LMR depots. A hydraulic set is seen at Huncoat, heading for Blackpool Central, passing another Cravens set. Despite being fitted with a four-character box, a two-digit code is still being used. *Colour-Rail*

Top: Between 1962 and 1967, 17 of the hydraulic vehicles were allocated to Cricklewood for use on the St Pancras–Bedford service. This allowed running over the City Widened Lines from which the longer Derby hydraulic units (Class 127s) were banned. They returned to Lancashire when all remaining Class 112s moved south. This hydraulic set is seen back on its original territory, heading for Skipton. As with the 150hp-engined cars, on DMBS vehicles the exhausts ran up through ducting in the van on the non-driver's side, while on DMCs it passed up the front of the toilet partition and here it can be seen coming through the roof. *Colour-Rail*

Above: The vehicles were prone to catching fire, some with serious consequences, resulting in several being written off which no doubt contributed to their early withdrawal. The gearbox sets went in November 1968, except for nine retained for Kentish Town–Barking services. Hydraulic sets were withdrawn in the first half of 1969 and the final vehicles from Cricklewood in November 1969. For a spell, some vehicles saw further use. Nos 51691 and 51692 became part of the BSC Shotton permanent way train and the front third of the bodyshell from No 51729 was apparently used as a store on an oil rig before becoming a paint store in a yard adjacent to the former Great Yarmouth South Town station. None was preserved. This set is seen at Skipton. *D. A. Hope/Colour-Rail*

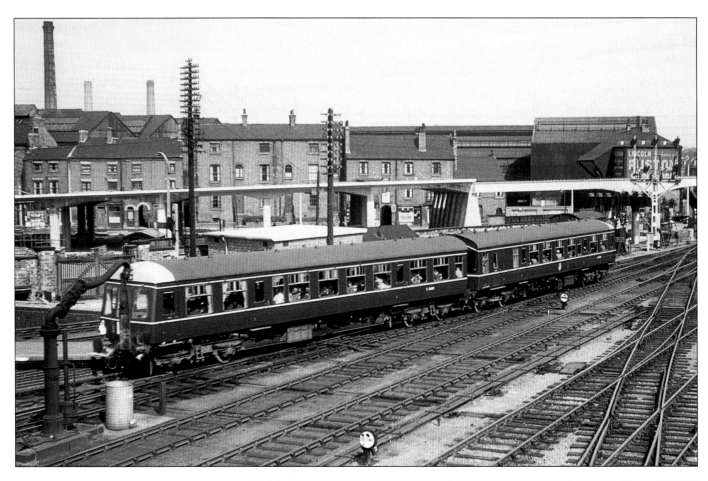

CLASS 114
Built by British Railways' Derby Works

Number	Type	Class	Seating	Weight	Diagram	Lot No
E50001-50048	DMBS	114	62	37½ tons	516	30209
E50049	DMBS	114	62	37½ tons	516	30459
E56001-56049	DTCL	148	12/62	29 10cwt tons	641	30210
Also:						
E50000	DMBS	-	62	41 tons 3cwt	632	30341
E56000	DTCL	-	12/62	31 tons 3cwt	641	30342

Original weight for 50001-50048 was 35½ tons when fitted with Leyland 150hp engines.

Above: Derby's first blue square units were 49 power/trailer sets in 1956 for ER Lincoln area services. These were also the first DMU vehicles to be built by Derby to use steel. Later nicknamed 'Derby Heavyweights', all but the final one were delivered with two Leyland 150hp engines. As they proved to be underpowered the last set was delivered with newly available Leyland Albion 230hp engines. This was a marked improvement, so the other vehicles were re-engined, starting in the summer of 1958. All were delivered to Lincoln, where this set is seen on 25 May 1957. The cleanliness of the body and roof paintwork gives the impression that this is a brand-new unit, although things below solebar level may say otherwise! One additional pair of vehicles (Nos E50000/E56000) was built with the same bodyshells, but with Rolls-Royce 238hp engines, hydraulic transmission and a different control system. It was, in effect, a testbed for the equipment that would be used in the Class 125 Lea Valley sets. It was withdrawn in October 1967, but would not have been classified as a Class 114.
M. Longdon/Colour-Rail

Above: Delivered in the pre-whiskers era, this set had had them added by 20 August 1959, when seen at New Holland Pier. Originally, there was only an upper marker light fitted and the blue squares seem to make up for the lack of lower lights by breaking up some of the empty space. This power car has been re-engined, identifiable by the long rectangular radiator with the curved top, rather than the original, small square version. *G. M. Staddon/Colour-Rail*

Above: Nos E56049 and E50049 are seen at Lincoln in June 1963 on a train to Boston. Freshly painted, it lacks a white dome. The yellow diagonal stripe on the coupling code is a variation that was used from time to time when a vehicle had minor differences, and the oval buffers were unusual for the class. *B. Nathan/Colour-Rail*

Below: At the start of Corporate blue era, the class appeared in the usual, small yellow panel and yellow cab door variations, before the livery was standardised, as on this set at Willoughby. The vehicles were refurbished, some appearing in the white with blue stripe livery before blue/grey took over. *Colour-Rail*

Above: The '114s' spent most of their lives working services in Lincolnshire, Humberside and the East Midlands, but did venture further away, such as this set seen at Peterborough, working to Cambridge on 26 March 1983, formed of Nos E50022 and E56023. The cab front has been modified, cleaning it up and standardising it with other classes, by removing the two-digit box and top light and fitting two lower marker lights which, by this period, would have been permissible to use as tail lights. *Colour-Rail*

Below: In 1984, Nos 53045 and 56004 were painted in a coffee and cream colour scheme to commemorate ten years of the South Yorkshire Passenger Transport Executive, and are seen at York in August that year. The introduction of 'Pacers' and 'Sprinters' in 1987 saw many of the units placed into store in Lincoln Holmes Yard. Late 1987 saw the transfer of the remaining passenger sets to Tyseley, where they widened their sphere of operations, but the fleet was gradually run down. By the end of 1991, only one set (T027) remained in traffic. In January 1992, No 54027 became due for overhaul and was taken out of use. No 53019 worked its final weeks in service coupled to Class 105 DTCL No 54484. *Colour-Rail*

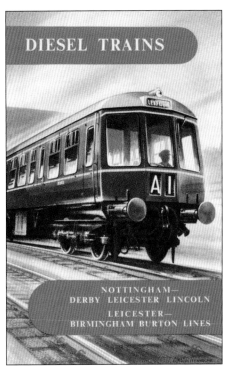

DIESEL TRAINS

NOTTINGHAM—
DERBY LEICESTER LINCOLN
LEICESTER—
BIRMINGHAM BURTON LINES

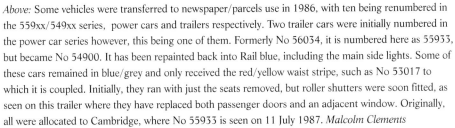

Above: Some vehicles were transferred to newspaper/parcels use in 1986, with ten being renumbered in the 559xx/549xx series, power cars and trailers respectively. Two trailer cars were initially numbered in the power car series however, this being one of them. Formerly No 56034, it is numbered here as 55933, but became No 54900. It has been repainted back into Rail blue, including the main side lights. Some of these cars remained in blue/grey and only received the red/yellow waist stripe, such as No 53017 to which it is coupled. Initially, they ran with just the seats removed, but roller shutters were soon fitted, as seen on this trailer where they have replaced both passenger doors and an adjacent window. Originally, all were allocated to Cambridge, where No 55933 is seen on 11 July 1987. *Malcolm Clements*

Above: The parcels sets moved to the Midlands but were all withdrawn by the end of 1990, except a pair that went into departmental use. Five vehicles are preserved. With a tail load, Nos 55931 and 54901 are seen on the last diagrammed Midlands DPU working, the 17.57 Manchester Piccadilly to Leeds mail at New Mills South Junction on 12 May 1990. *Kevin Dowd*

Number	Type	Class	Seats	Weight	Diagram	Lot No
M51651-51680	DMBS	115	78	38 tons	598	30530
M51849-51860	DMBS	115	78	38 tons	598	30595
M51861-51900	DMBS	115	78	38 tons	598	30598
M59649-59663	TS	173	106	29 tons	590	30531
M59664-59678	TCL	177	30/40	30 tons	599	30532
M59713-59718	TS	173	106	29 tons	590	30596
M59719-59724	TCL	177	30/40	30 tons	599	30597
M59725-59744	TS	173	106	29 tons	590	30599
M59745-59764	TCL	177	30/40	30 tons	599	30600

Below left: The Marylebone–High Wycombe–Princes Risborough diesel scheme was not just about new trains, it included alterations to stations, buildings and tracks. The new sets were ready before the route, so initial deliveries saw them join the similar Rolls-Royce sets working from St Pancras, while later cars were put into storage. Differences between the '115s' and the '127s' were the underframe equipment, most notably the size and location of the radiators. The Albion engines were easily visible on the '115s', less so on the '127s'. Both types had very high-backed seating compared with other suburban designs, and both types were ungangwayed four-car sets with a DMBS at both ends, a TS and either a TSL ('127s') or TCL ('115s'). A set is seen here at West Ruislip on a down local. *Colour-Rail*

Below: The sets seen here at Aylesbury Town on 3 July 1966 look very smart, now with yellow panels. The station appears to be doing good business in parcels traffic. This was one of the main destinations to which these DMUs worked to from Marylebone; others included High Wycombe and Banbury. Six sets were allocated to the Liverpool area for the CLC route to Manchester, initially working in pairs as eight-car sets on an hourly express service between the two cities. They later joined the rest of the class at Marylebone. *Colour-Rail*

Top: The sets were refurbished, many appearing in the white/blue stripe colours before blue and grey. This view shows blue/grey TS No M59650. In 1987, there were some major shuffles to the LMR DMU fleet, and Tyseley gained 22 power cars and a number of trailer cars that enabled a fleet of four-car sets to be formed for the Cross City line. Also that year, some DMBSs were gangwayed and paired with Class 108 DTCs (as pictured earlier). *Malcolm Clements*

Above: Over the years, the sets had a variety of buffers including cut, oval and large round, as seen here. In 1981, some power cars were fitted with sanding gear to aid adhesion, and sand boxes can be seen on the side of the bogies of this DMBS at Marylebone in June 1989. The Marylebone sets, which were later transferred to Bletchley, but remained on Chiltern Line duties, were declared surplus after the introduction of Class 165s from 1991 onwards. While at Bletchley depot, the class was also used on the Barking to Gospel Oak line, units being formed as power twins, until replaced by Class 117 power twins. The final Class 115 working out of Marylebone was in July 1992, the Tyseley sets surviving a little longer, until February 1994. Many vehicles are now in preservation. *Colour-Rail*

CLASS 116
Built by British Railways, Derby Works

Above: The first high-density suburban sets were these Derby triple sets and three batches were built, totalling 320 vehicles. As with other suburban coaching stock, they were intended for short-distance commuter runs, so many doors were fitted to allow masses of passengers to board and alight quickly. Toilets were not deemed necessary, neither were gangways. Internal partitions, mainly used to divide the interior into smoking and non-smoking sections, meant bodyside lights were split into two where these were located. Only the DMBSs originally had doors through the partitions. Following the same rules as for locomotive-hauled coaches, being suburban stock, they were not originally lined out. Early deliveries did not have whiskers, but these were added later, as seen on this set at Lapworth, heading for Wellington. Using 150hp Leyland engines, all were new to the Western Region, being first introduced on 17 June 1957 in the Birmingham area. *Colour-Rail*

Number	Type	Class	Seats (New/gangwayed)	Weight	Diagram (New/gangwayed)	Lot No	Year
W50050-50091	DMBS	116/2	65 2nd	36 tons	553/853	30211	1957
W50092-50133	DMS	116/1	95/89 2nd	36 tons	554/854	30213	1957
W50818-50870	DMBS	116/2	65 2nd	36 tons	553/853	30363	1957/58
W50871-50923	DMS	116/1	95/89 2nd	36 tons	554/854	30364	1957/58
W51128-51140	DMBS	116/2	65 2nd	36 tons	553/853	30446	1958
W51141-51153	DMS	116/1	95/89 2nd	36 tons	554/854	30447	1958
W59000-59031	TC	175	28/20 1st + 74/68 2nd	28 tons 10cwt	555/855	30212	1957
W59032-59041	TS	172	106/98 2nd	29 tons	600/856	30385	1957
W59326-59376	TC	175	28/20 1st + 74/68 2nd	28 tons 10cwt	555/855	30365	1957/58
W59438-59448	TC	175	28/20 1st + 74/68 2nd	28 tons 10cwt	555/855	30448	1958

Above: These vehicles will always be known for their work on South Wales valley services. First introduced on 2 December 1957 to the majority of Eastern and Western valley services between Newport and Blaenavon and Newport, Brynmawr and Ebbw Vale (Low Level), workings were expanded to the Cardiff Valleys in January 1958, taking over more and more services as vehicles were delivered. This set is seen at Senghenydd on 27 July 1963. *Colour-Rail*

Above left: The first batch of vehicles had the four-lamp arrangement, the later ones receiving a two-character headcode box below the centre cab window, with just two lamps, one either side, as seen on No W50846, now with a yellow warning panel. *Colour-Rail*

Left: Some of the '116s' were lined out, such as No M51144 seen at Moor Street on 2 August 1967. Of interest now are the period cars, including a Ford Anglia, BMC 1200, Morris Oxford, Austin Cambridge, Morris Minor and a Scammell Scarab! *Colour-Rail*

Above: The two-digit route indicator identifies the DMS from set No C319 as being from batch two or three. It is seen as a two-car set coming off the Looe branch at Liskeard, in the company of a GRCW Cross-Country set on a Branch Line Society special. There is a red flag on the track on the opposite line. *Colour-Rail*

Left: Line closures on the WR resulted in surplus sets and in 1970, the first regional transfers of the class took place. With PayTrain operation now introduced, nine non-gangwayed three-car sets were selected from Cardiff, Bristol and Plymouth for the ScR (Hamilton). Another seven went to the ER for services from Liverpool Street, based at Stratford (SF). One of the Stratford sets, with No 50828 at the rear, is seen heading for Cambridge in July 1974. The two-digit box has been plated over and the first-class area can be clearly seen. The smoking and non-smoking sections have been swapped, giving more non-smoking rather than smoking, reflecting the change in social attitudes since the vehicles were built. *Colour-Rail*

Left: The '116s' were selected for refurbishment, although not all vehicles were treated. Set No TS500 is one that had been through the process, and is seen here at Bewdley on an experimental BR Kidderminster–Bewdley service in August 1979. At this time, southbound SVR trains terminated at Bewdley as part of the line to Kidderminster was still in BR use for sugar beet traffic. The shuttle was a success and became a regular event for special galas, often running through to Birmingham New Street. It continued until the end of 1983 when the remaining section of line was acquired, allowing SVR trains to run into a new station at Kidderminster in the 1984 season. *K. Bannister/Colour-Rail*

Above: The class remained part of the Scottish scene for many years, and two vehicles are seen here in a hybrid set with a Class 107 vehicle, on a Kilmacolm service. The '116' DMBS is also likely to be carrying the GG Trans-Clyde logo on the driver's side, as per the '107'. The Kilmacolm branch closed in January 1983, with a loss of DMU duties, although part of the line re-opened a few years later as far as Paisley Canal. An unusual variation on the blue/grey livery appeared on a set in 1985 when Tyseley extended the grey (with white lines) forward over the driver's doors and round to meet black cab window surrounds. It carried the WM logo on the front. *Colour-Rail*

Above right: In 1985, the Valley Trains branding was launched. The vehicles were adorned with a red V and a dragon on the front, and 'Trên y Cwm' and 'Valley Train' on opposite sides, with double arrows and a dragon. So adorned is set No C375, containing Nos 53855, 59561 and 53908. *Colour-Rail*

Right: Numbers dwindled over the years, but with such a large class the '116s' managed to last into the NSE era. The surviving top headlight mount seems to make No 53083 look very dated in this view at Didcot North Junction. It is working with '101' driver trailer No 54381 on 20 June 1991. Final withdrawals were in 1995 and eleven vehicles entered preservation. *Colour-Rail*

CLASS 117
Built by Pressed Steel

Above: The Western wanted more suburban sets, but British Railways' own workshops were at capacity so an order was put out to tender, this eventually being split between Pressed Steel and BRCW. The order placed in October 1958 totalled 168 vehicles: 57 DMBSs, 57 DMSs and 54 TCs. BRCW built 45 vehicles for 15 sets — the '118s', Pressed Steel the remainder — the '117s' in 1959/60. Of these, 108 vehicles were for suburban services from Paddington, 15 for the Bristol–Taunton area and 45 for services in Devon and Cornwall, west of Newton Abbot. British Railways supplied the drawings to both companies which were basically an updated version of Derby's own suburban vehicles (the '116s') again with 150hp Leyland engines. The seating can be clearly seen in this view; these originally being maroon with tan headrests. As with the '116s', the '117s' were at first painted under coaching stock rules and so were unlined, but after protest from the WR General Manager, deliveries from the 20th set onwards were lined out before leaving the Linwood works. One of the unlined sets is seen at Ruscombe on 21 April 1962.
L. E. Elsey/Colour-Rail

Top right: The '117' sets included toilets and, although ungangwayed when built, these were added from 1965, mainly to allow PayTrain operation. When yellow panels were added, it made the lack of marker lights on the cab front more obvious: they were added in later years. Another change was the buffers — built with the 'cut' version, these were later replaced by the large round type. As with the '116s', the exhausts originally joined together at the rear of the power car, being emitted through a single box above where the corridor would have been. No W51364 is seen heading an Oxford service at Kidlington, on 11 November 1964. *Colour-Rail*

Above right: DMUs were popular for certain railtours as they could easily travel over branch lines without the inconvenience of a locomotive requiring to be run round at the destination. Here, with not a yellow vest in sight, set No L420 has gained a Met-Camm TC. With blue livery, the vehicle numbering font changed to 'Rail Alphabet', but WR kept set numbers on the cab fronts in Gill Sans. The handrail is still of the hollow type acting as a drain. *Colour-Rail*

Number	Type	Class	Seats		Weight	Diagram		Lot No
			(New/gangwayed)			(New/Gangwayed)		
W51332-51373	DMBS	117/2	65/65 2nd		36 tons	534/850		30546
W51374-51415	DMS	117/1	91/89 2nd		36 tons	535/852		30548
W59484-59522	TCL	176	24/22 1st; 50/48 2nd		30 tons	601/851		30547

Right: These vehicles went through the refurbishment scheme, being turned out in the white/blue stripe livery, but most were still without marker lights. By the time they appeared in blue/grey, all cars had the lights fitted. The bodyside grille just in front of the van doors was an intake for the heater, which had been moved up from below solebar level in an attempt to eliminate heater exhaust fumes being drawn into the vehicle. This had been a long-term problem with DMUs, particularly when standing at a platform.
Set No L413 is seen entering Reading in August 1986. *Colour-Rail*

Above: In 1985, Bristol-based set No B430 (Nos W51368 + W59520 + W51410) was selected for painting in chocolate and cream for GW150 celebrations, although it carried BR coaching crests rather than the GWR logo, so actually represented British Railways Western Region livery. A single car (No 55020) was also so treated. The set subsequently became No T305, then No 117305 and was popular for open days and railtours and it is seen far from home at Carlisle on 22 October 1988. *Colour-Rail*

Right: One of the easiest ways to distinguish '117s' from '118s' was by the headcode box. The BRCW units all had curved tops, the Pressed Steel sets had a flatter top, *except* the first few delivered, as evident in this picture of No 51335 on 22 April 1992. It carries NSE livery with a Thames logo on the van. *Colour-Rail*

Right: The class was amongst the last of the first-generation sets to remain in service. They were 'facelifted' at Doncaster, emerging in the Regional Railways colour scheme and here, set No 117314 (Nos 51352 + 59489 + 51394) is seen awaiting release from Doncaster Works, during the open day on 12 July 1992. Their final days were spent based at Bletchley and Haymarket. The ScR sets operated the Fife Circle services, from Edinburgh to Edinburgh via Dunfermline/Kirkcaldy in peak periods only, together with a single run to Perth and back. They were not favoured by commuters, and late in 1999 they were reduced to two-car sets. Soon after, once the arrival of the Class 170s allowed cascading of 'Sprinters', they were taken out of use at very short notice. Three vehicles remain on the network, as a water jetting train for Chiltern Railways, and many are in preservation. *Kevin Dowd*

CLASS 118
Built by Birmingham Railway Carriage & Wagon

Number	Type	Class	Seats (New/gangwayed)		Weight	Diagram (New/gangwayed)	Lot No	Year
W51302-51316	DMBS	118/2	65 2nd		36 tons	534/850	30543	1960
W51317-51331	DMS	118/1	91/89 2nd		36 tons	535/852	30545	1960
W59469-59483	TCL	174	24/22 1st;	50/48 2nd	30 tons	601/851	30544	1960

Left: All the BRCW sets had the curved headcode box top and all are believed to have been lined when delivered, but not all had lamps when new! Although there were 15 vehicles of each type delivered, it was not unknown for them to run as two-car sets, as in this view of No W51320 and partner at Falmouth. *L. E. Elsey/Colour-Rail*

Below: No W51330 was delivered with lamps and is seen here at Fareham in August 1961. The aluminium window surrounds enhance the front edge and the design of the frames gave an unpainted area for easy removal of the retaining rubbers when changing windows. This vehicle was destroyed in a fire at Cardiff Canton in June 1992. *Colour-Rail*

Above: In plain blue with the distinctive WR Gill Sans set number, B477 is seen at Bridport on 2 May 1977. Note the figure 1s on first-class doors of the centre car. The 150hp Leyland-engines vehicles were allocated to Plymouth Laira (LA), Bristol (BR) and Reading (RG) and latterly to Cardiff Canton (CF) and Birmingham Tyseley (TS). *Colour-Rail*

Below: Here is No W51312 in blue livery at St Budeaux (Victoria Road) on 10 March 1979. When the four-character route indicator became obsolete, some '118s' had the two white dots fitted to this, as was the style on locomotives. These acted as marker lights, the vehicle lacking the normal type of marker lights fitted when the cab fronts were standardised. Note also the lack of blue squares. *Colour-Rail*

Above: By far the most unusual and distinctive set (of any type?) was No P460, repainted to advertise British Telecom. The driver's side of the power cars read 'It's Telecom on the line', from which a squiggly line ran along the centre car to 'Making fast connections' on the non-driving side of the other power car. Launched in February 1985, it is seen on a Laira shuttle on 7 September 1985. The same year saw the first of the class withdrawn, after surviving 25 years without any casualties. *Mel Holley/Colour-Rail*

Left: As with many high-density sets, Tyseley latterly gained an allocation of '118s'. Set No T316 consists here of Nos 51306, 59473 and 51321, seen at Cardiff Central. There is a lack of roof vents. These cars had previously been set Nos P464 and B464 and were transferred to Tyseley in 1988. The two power cars became Sandite sets in 1991 and No 51321 was subsequently preserved as the sole survivor of the class. Some vehicles carried Valley brandings in blue/grey and No 51319 at least, was painted in NSE colours before they were finally withdrawn from passenger use in 1994. *Colour-Rail*

CLASS 119
Built by Gloucester Railway
Carriage & Wagon

Numbers	Type	Class	Seats	Weight	Diagram	Lot No
W51052-51079	DMBC	119/1	18/16	36 tons 19cwt	540	30421
W51080-51107	DMSL	119/2	68	37 tons 10cwt	541	30422
W59413-59437	TSBL	178	60	31 tons 8cwt	542	30423

Above: GRCW won a contract to build 28 Cross-Country sets that Swindon could not undertake. As these were built straight after their single-unit cars from 1958, the firm was given concessions to use the construction jigs they already had. The underframe layout was based on the 'bubblecars' rather than the Swindon sets; the body framework followed the Derby design, and of course, the Derby cab was used. However, the bodyside and interior layout remained Swindon style, so the vehicles were a strange combination of the two works' designs. Smaller external differences also help to identify the two types: at the gangway end corners the GRCW gutter was distinctly angled, and Gloucester was about twice as generous with its roof vents as Swindon. Swindon preferred curtains at first and second-class windows, but GRCW thought blinds were good enough for second-class. This picture shows that first-class did get antimacassars though! The footsteps are on the right-hand side of the gangway on the centre car — Swindon had these on the left. This view of a set at Norton Junction shows how nice GRCW's interpretation of whiskers was, being much narrower, having rounded ends, and neatly leading down to the vacuum pipes. *Michael Mensing/Colour-Rail*

Above: No W51068 has received a yellow panel in this view at Calne on 2 June 1965. Note the white window on the staff door to the buffet on the centre car. The AEC-engined (later Leyland) sets worked on many duties throughout the Western Region, on true cross-country services, often paired with the Swindon type, and occasionally with the addition of a converted Hawksworth coach for extra capacity to form a four-car train. They were equally at home working on lesser lines, and were regulars on many now-closed branches such as Bridport and Minehead, as well as Calne. From new they were associated with Bristol–Weymouth services. *Colour-Rail*

Above: A few vehicles appeared in the plain blue/small yellow panel livery, but in general, their Cross-Country status allowed them to skip plain blue and receive blue/grey. With Wolverhampton High Level on the blinds, Nos 51102, 59430 and 51073 sit at Chester General on 7 September 1969. *Colour-Rail*

Right: Some sets were given a refurbishment that included converting part of the van and the now-obsolete buffet area to additional luggage storage. These sets were then dedicated to Reading–Gatwick services and could be identified by the red labels proclaiming 'Passenger Luggage Stowage Area' at these areas. The cab front has had the two-digit box plated over. *Colour-Rail*

Right: The only other livery the class carried was Network SouthEast, and in common with other types, the NSE branding was carried on the centre car, with a Thames logo on the van and buffet. A NSE-liveried set had the red line painted into blue when it moved to Tyseley as No T575 in an attempt to look more like Regional Railways colours! Most of the class was withdrawn by 1988, but a few carried on, some lasting until 1995. Three vehicles survive in preservation, but unfortunately there are no centre cars. *Colour-Rail*

Numbers	Type	Class	Seating	Weight	Diagram	Lot No	Year
W50647-50695	DMSL	120/2	68	36 tons 10cwt	586	30334	1958
W50696-50744	DMBC	120/1	18/16	36 tons	587	30335	1958
W51573-51581	DMBC	120/1	18/16	36 tons 7cwt	636	30515	1961
W51582-51590	DMSL	120/2	68	36 tons 10cwt	637	30516	1961
Sc51781-51787	DMBC	120/1	18/16	36 tons 7cwt	587	30559	1959
Sc51788-51794	DMSL	120/2	68	36 tons 10cwt	586	30560	1959
W59255-59301	TSLRB	179	60	31 tons	561	30336	1958
W59579-59588	TSL	179	68	30 tons 12cwt	572	30517	1961
Sc59679-59685	TSLRB	179	60	30 tons 12cwt	561	30561	1959

Top: We finally come across vehicles from the final first-generation railcar builder to be found in this book, British Railways' own Swindon Works. These were Cross-Country triple sets powered by 150 AEC engines and, built in three batches: 49 sets in 1958 for the WR, seven sets in 1959 for the ScR, and a further nine sets in 1961 for the WR. The distinctive Cross-Country features were a large guard's van and a small buffet in the centre cars. Unlike many other types that put first-class seating in an unpowered coach, reducing noise and vibration to enhance passenger comfort, Swindon put the first-class into a power car. With this and the large van area there was only room for two second-class seating bays in this coach! Swindon liked to have the waist and upper lining the same thickness while Derby used a thinner top line. The same cab front as the earlier build of the 79xxx Inter-City type was used, but it did not look as austere with the stencil headcode replaced by four lamps and a destination indicator. Two six-car sets from the first batch are seen at Locking Road on 9 December 1959. *Colour-Rail*

Above: The first two batches were very similar, but by the time the third batch was built, the four-digit route indicator had replaced the four-lamp arrangement, and looked somewhat cumbersome. Oddly, one marker light remained. The first batch had round buffers, the second were 'cut', although ovals soon became common. Some cars carried different types on the same bufferbeam! The third batch had ovals. This batch also differed by not having a buffet section, the centre cars being Trailer Seconds. Peculiarly, there were ten trailers in the third batch, one more than the number of sets built. Some of these faced early withdrawal in 1967, when less than seven years old and were cut up by Woodham's at Barry, which was unusual for DMU cars. What was not unusual, despite the extra centre cars, was running as power twins, such as this set leaving Barnstaple Town on an up Ilfracombe service in May 1966. *Colour-Rail*

Above: Like the GRCW Cross-Country sets, the WR cars went straight into blue/grey livery, with the exception of a few that appeared in plain blue with a small yellow panel. The class was first introduced in 1958, replacing the Inter-City sets on the Birmingham–South Wales runs, and also starting on Cardiff–Bristol services. As the number of sets grew, so did their use on other lines on the region. This set is seen at Hartlebury, heading for Birmingham. The '120s' were unique amongst the Swindon builds in having WR suspended gangways and screw-link couplings, the others having Pullman gangways and buckeyes. As well as brackets for sideboards, all Swindon cars had brackets for coach letters, and these were occasionally seen in use. *T. Nall/Colour-Rail*

Above: One of the WR sets was loaned to the ScR in 1958, working the Aberdeen–Inverness and Glasgow–Oban lines to judge suitability. The outcome was the eventual takeover of the former route by this class. The Oban line remained locomotive-hauled, although the sets did work some of the additional summer services. These seven sets were the only DMUs fitted with tablet catchers, inset on the rear luggage van doors, and some of these were still fitted as late as 1979. As if the van was not big enough already on these sets, four of the DMBCs had the second-class area converted to additional storage space, making them DMBFs. The ScR '120s' became plain blue in the late 1960s, rather than blue/grey. Around the same time, some GRCW single cars were allocated to the Scottish line, and it was not uncommon to see them tagged on to the end of a Cross-Country set. This set is at Keith Junction, heading for Aberdeen. Ahead on the right, can be seen the line for Dufftown, part of which is now a heritage railway. *Colour-Rail*

Above: Some vehicles went through the asbestos stripping and refurbishment process, but apparently the different method of internal fitting out made this very expensive, so this was not progressed in full. However, most cars received some sort of facelift and a few were given B4 bogies. From 1964, six two-car units operated the Central Wales line. These sets were fitted with a headlamp, mounted between the two cab windows, for safety reasons, because of the many level crossings. This set, on a Shrewsbury service, is seen with no less than six lamps on the back end! Met-Camms were introduced to the line in 1984. *Colour-Rail*

Right: The LMR gained sets from the mid-1960s, starting with 22 moving to Derby Etches Park, which retained a sizeable allocation for two decades. From there, they covered a wide range of duties, mainly on the Lincoln-Crewe line and associated services to Grantham, Leicester, Birmingham and Matlock. In the twilight years, set No EP522 (formed of Nos 53714, 59293 and 53678) is seen at Derby on 24 November 1984. Other LMR depots with '120' allocations included Chester (working to Manchester, Crewe, North Wales, Shrewsbury and the Cambrian Coast) and Newton Heath (mainly for Blackpool services). Many sets had alternative trailers, mainly Met-Camms. *Mel Holley*

Centre right: Some LMR vehicles were converted for parcels use, one of which is seen here. This is No 51782, a former ScR DMBF conversion, which is identifiable by the two missing windows in the centre of the vehicle. Only one was removed on the opposite side. It is paired with Class 116 DMBS No 53072 at Leeds on 27 June 1986; both cars are carrying the Red Star logo. *Malcolm Clements*

Below right: The introduction of 'Sprinters' to the LMR saw the '120s' become surplus. At the same time, the ScR was having problems with Class 107s, so the class made a return to Scottish workings, starting off on Ayrshire services, but were soon appearing on most Central Belt DMU duties. This set is seen at Dunblane in 1988, containing a Met-Camm centre car. Both power cars have had the majority of roof vents removed, leaving just one at either end. Scottish sets also appeared with the cab window surrounds in black with a few carrying 'ScotRail' branding on the bodyside. The last of the class were withdrawn in October 1989. Just one vehicle survives in preservation — a buffet centre car. *Andrew McConnell*

CLASS 121
Built by Pressed Steel

Above: The GRCW '122' single cars proved successful, so a further batch was ordered, this time from Pressed Steel and delivered in 1960/61. While the '122s' were basically '116' DMBSs with a cab at the back end, the '121s' were '117s' with the extra cab. Again, some trailer cars were built for strengthening where required. The single cars have proved to be the most versatile of the first-generation fleet, being able to work solo or with a trailer, be tagged on to a set, or substitute for a power car in a set. Beyond passenger service there has been parcels use and they proved ideal for use as route learning and Sandite cars. Recent years have seen the '121s' become camera units and Severn Tunnel vehicles and, after some years of absence, returning to passenger use after major overhauls and upgrading to present-day safety standards. They have also carried more liveries than any other first-generation type, with many one-off colour schemes in later years. Here, No 55029 is seen at Staines West on 7 May 1961, at the time about six months old. It is fitted with oval buffers; some had the 'cut' type from new, and latterly, all had large round ones. *Colour-Rail*

Above right: Now with a yellow panel, No W55028 is seen stabled with a trailer car. They were fitted with WR ATC, which involved additional pipework, which is visible going from the solebar to the faraway bogie. Unlike the '117s', they were fitted with AEC engines from new, being changed later to Leylands. The first 25 years of service was solely on the Western Region, concentrated around the Reading, Bristol, Cardiff and Plymouth areas, and use on the West London branch lines, the Severn Beach branch, lines in the Welsh valleys, and the Cornish branch lines. *D. A. Hope/Colour-Rail*

Right: This vehicle, seen at Liskeard, is in plain blue with a WR Gill Sans set number. On this class, the set numbers reflected the vehicle number, '129' being No W55029. The prominent driver's handrail is still the hollow type. *Colour-Rail*

Numbers	Type	Class	Seats	Weight	Diagram	Lot No
W55020-55035	DMBS	121	65	37 tons 8cwt	512	30518
W56280-56289	DTS	149	93 (89 gangwayed)	29 tons 7cwt	513 (513A gangwayed)	30519

Above: Only this pair of vehicles appeared in refurbished livery, Nos W55034 (L134) and trailer No W56283. *Colour-Rail*

Below: Most single units went straight into blue/grey, as did No W55033 seen at Swindon Works on 5 October 1980. This vehicle received a replacement roof dome at the exhaust end, one without the headcode box, but it has the smaller destination box. This made the vehicle easily identifiable from the others, although the same mismatched end appeared on GRCW car No 55005 which ended up with Pressed Steel exhausts! Noticeable in this view is the heater air intake grille which appeared on the bodyside, just above the number. *Colour-Rail*

Top right: There were countless variations in blue/grey. No W55032 is seen here with set No T405 on a railtour at Weymouth Quay, with the Valley Train markings on the cab. The double arrows are of different sizes on the two vehicles; the larger type was also carried on some '121s'. At least one vehicle had an arrow replaced by a NSE logo, but the strangest adornment was on No 55026 which spent some time working in the Bristol area with an Inverness Highland Rail stag logo in the middle of the cab front! *K. Bannister/Colour-Rail*

Bottom right: No W55020 was painted in chocolate and cream for the GW150 celebrations and, in common with the '117' set treated similarly, the BR coaching crest was used. The type of roof vents can be seen here; the GRCW cars differed in having shell vents. About to enter a station on an Ealing Broadway–Greenford working on 5 September 1986, note that half the passenger doors are already open before the platform is reached! *Colour-Rail*

Above: No 55023 was painted back into green to commemorate what was thought to be at the time the last Class 121 overhaul. With a headlight now added, the vehicle is captured at Bletchley about to work the 11.50 Bletchley to Bedford on 4 August 1993. *Colour-Rail*

Right: There were two variations to NSE livery; No 55022 is seen here in April 1988 with the ends of the colour bands swept up.

Below right: This formation of 121/TCL/121, seen in June 1992, has a straight-ended version of the NSE livery, and a smaller logo at the end rather than in the centre. Many other liveries followed, such as Silverlink, Midline, Maroon, Railtrack brown, Railtrack lime green/purple, yellow and South West Trains. At the time of writing, one vehicle is in traffic in Chiltern Railways blue on the Aylesbury–Princes Risborough branch and a second has just been refurbished for Arriva Trains Wales for operation on Cardiff Bay shuttles. A further seven vehicles are in preservation (including three trailers). *Colour-Rail*

Numbers	Type	Class	Seats	Weight	Diagram	Lot No
W55000-55019	DMBS	122	65	36 tons	539	30419
W56291-56299	DTS	150	95 — later reduced to 91	29 tons	538	304200

Above: The GRCW Co Ltd built 20 of these single-unit railcars in 1958 , to designs drawn up by Derby C&W works, and they were effectively a Class 116 DMBS (the high-density sets then in production at Derby), with a cab at both ends. Along with the later Pressed Steel type, they were nicknamed 'bubblecars'. Their main purpose was use in the Birmingham and London areas of the WR, including taking over from many of the GWR railcars. Trailer cars were built for these vehicles, for use when loadings required, as in this view of a pair entering West Ealing. The two exhaust pipes joining and emitting through a single box was in fact common on many Derby-built/designed units, it just was not normally visible! The van end was regarded as the rear of the vehicle, and so all the data normally found on the back of vehicles can be seen on the left side of the cab. *K. Bannister/Colour-Rail*

Left: This vehicle now has a yellow panel and is seen at Norton Fitzwarren on 19 May 1965. Compare this with the picture of the Class 116 in this livery at Moor Street. The GRCW cars could be identified by the thicker top line. *Colour-Rail*

Above: As lines closed, transfers saw the vehicles operating services in Bristol, Cornwall and Plymouth, including many services on former SR lines to Gunnislake and Barnstaple. This car is seen at Fowey in plain blue. The exhausts no longer join at the top. *Colour-Rail*

Left: In the late 1960s some vehicles were reallocated to Scotland, three being converted to parcels cars, officially becoming Class 131 DMLVs. This formation contains two three-car Met-Camms, a parcels car and a van and is seen passing Carricknowe on a Stirling–Edinburgh working on 21 May 1971. As can be seen, the Gloucester car has had most of the windows painted white and is in the early variation of plain blue livery with small yellow panels. *G. M. Staddon*

Left: The ScR passenger vehicles were used in the Glasgow, Ayrshire, Edinburgh and Dundee areas and also became common on the Aberdeen–Inverness line, normally tagged on to the end of a Class 120 set, but in this case, one is substituting for a DMBC at Aberdeen, on 25 March 1978. *G. M. Staddon*

Right: The other WR cars, except No 55001 which went into departmental use in 1969, were cascaded to the West Midlands (based at Tyseley) and used on local services, most notably the Leamington Spa to Stratford upon Avon route. This pair is seen at Leamington Spa, on the 11.50 from Stratford upon Avon. The arrow sizes are different and one car has the WM logo Like the '121s', they were built with AEC engines but later switched to Leylands.
P. Hutchinson/Colour-Rail

Below right: In 1987, problems with Class 142 units on the West Country branches resulted in a belated reprieve for six cars. Their diagrams in the West Midlands were rearranged and they were sent south via Vic Berry's yard in Leicester for asbestos removal. The cars then worked the Cornish branch lines to Looe, Newquay and St Ives, until withdrawal. Here, Nos 55012 and 55003 are seen at Barnstaple on 13 April 1992, the former in Regional Railways colours. This was one of the last passenger vehicles to be withdrawn, in December 1993, and it went into departmental use as a route learner for Loadhaul, being painted in their colours. *Colour-Rail*

Below: More than half the class went into departmental use over the years, mainly as route learners. Some had the destination box removed from the roof dome, and painted into an olive livery. The once-solid partition in the van now has windows so that staff in training can observe the route. This view was taken at York in July 1979. At the time of writing, there are six vehicles in preservation (no trailers), and one is still in use as a sandite/route learner. *Colour-Rail*

CLASS 123
Built by British Railways, Swindon Works

Numbers	Type	Class	Seats	Weight	Diagram	Lot No
W52086-52095	DMBS(L)	123/2	32	41 tons	566	30703
W52096-52105	DMSK(L)	123/1	64	42 tons	574	30704
W59235-59239	TS(L)	182	64	31 tons	568	30706
W59818-59827	TCK(L)	183	24/24	32 tons	567	30705
W59828-59832	TSRB	184	32	35 tons	569	30707

Above: These were the final batch of first-generation units and were built by BR Swindon in 1963 and, as with the first DMUs it built back in 1956, they were designated as Inter-City sets. There were 10 four-car sets, half having buffets. Gangways at the outer ends of the sets allowed a buffet set to be attached to a non-buffet set giving access throughout. They were very attractive units in green. They missed the whiskers period, being delivered in the yellow panel era, and the yellow gangway cover was a nice way of tackling this, with the white dome, a first for Swindon vehicles, really setting it off. Handrails can be seen along the passenger windows on No W52066, a compartment vehicle with a side corridor. The electrical conduit which runs below solebar level is identifiable by the occasional orange band. As it has buckeye couplings (painted blue), retractable buffers are fitted as on normal coaching stock, with an adjacent mount for the saddle when not in use. *Colour-Rail DE1528*

Above right: The early part of their lives was unsettled, never truly finding a home. They were introduced in 1963 between Swansea, Cardiff, Birmingham, Derby and Crewe, and appeared on the Cardiff to Bristol route. Displacement saw them allocated to Reading for working outer-suburban services out of Paddington to Oxford and Newbury. Three sets are seen here at Reading on the 12.14 to Paddington on 23 March 1971. The next move was to Cardiff for working secondary services from South Wales, such as to Bristol. They were then put into store at Barry in 1977 as the WR had no further use for them. The buffet cars had been withdrawn in 1970 although one, No 59831, became part of a Class 309 EMU set as No 69108 to replace an accident-damaged vehicle. *Colour-Rail*

Right: The ER saw the potential in the vehicles, as they were similar to their Trans-Pennine units, with the same mechanical components, and they moved to Hull. Mixed with the '124s', the sets worked the South Trans-Pennine route, Hull–Doncaster–Sheffield–Manchester and occasionally to Leeds. They were not refurbished, but still passed through works as required. The DMBS pictured at Doncaster in May 1981 appears to be recently ex-works, although the other vehicles in the set do not. The bogies identify the types of vehicles, the '123' being the only type to get B4s, so the formation is 123 DMBS/124 TS/123 TCK/124 DMC. On the '123' power cars the extent of the grey varied, some including the door next to the cab, others not. Some carried the Trans-Pennine branding on the side. The route indicator boxes have gone, replaced by marker lights, the gangway cover is missing, and the inner door appears to be sealed. Despite being tidied up, the front end has lost all the charm it had when new. Their last workings were in May 1984, and none survives. *Colour-Rail*

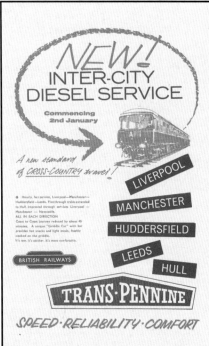

Above: The Trans-Pennine sets are generally regarded as the most handsome DMUs built and this is due to the heavy influence of the BR Design Panel and consultant Ted Wilkes. The formation was almost identical to the 1956 Inter-City sets on the Edinburgh–Glasgow route, but the Trans-Pennine sets were unique in having intermediate power cars without cabs. The four Albion-engined power cars gave the six-car sets what they needed to tackle the severe gradients on the line. Introduced in January 1961, early days saw the distinctive 'Trans-Pennine' headboard carried, and four vehicles also carried sideboards. *Colour-Rail*

Numbers	Type	Class	Seats	Weight	Diagram	Lot No
E51951-51967	DMC	124/1	21/36	40 tons	577	30603
E51968-51984	MBSL	124/2	48	41 tons	579	30604
E59765-59773	TSL	180	64	32 tons	573	30605
E59774-59781	TFBL	181	18 + 8 buffet	34 tons	562	30606

Above: Despite being delivered well into the whiskers period, these having been added for safety reasons, it is perhaps surprising that these units did not have them when new. No E51952 has had a yellow panel added when seen at Stalybridge in 1966. There is no headboard, but some tangerine-coloured sideboards are still carried. (Did the driver not realise that the headcode blinds are seen in the opposite order from what he sees in the cab?) Their main duties were on Hull–Liverpool and Leeds–Manchester–Liverpool services. *Colour-Rail*

Right: With headcodes now no longer required to be carried, the blinds on this set are wound to display four dots. Reduced to a four-car formation, this set, including No 51963, is seen at Leeds on 24 April 1976. The buffet cars had all been withdrawn by 1975. The class never appeared in plain blue, but at least one blue/grey vehicle had yellow cab doors. *Colour-Rail*

Right: In the late 1970s, services were revamped, some going over to locomotive hauled, and the sets were to be concentrated on Hull–Manchester/South Humberside services. Joined by the WR Inter-City sets, the mixed formations worked on services such as Manchester Piccadilly to Cleethorpes via Sheffield, Doncaster and Barnetby. No E51952 is seen at Manchester Piccadilly with a Class 123 vehicle behind. The route indicator has now been plated over and fitted with marker/tail lamps and the handrails are picked out in white. The cab also carries the number 52, reflecting the vehicle number. 'Trans-Pennine' was hand-painted on the sides of some power cars. In 1981, the intermediate power cars were converted to become trailers and the final vehicles were withdrawn in May 1984; none survives. *Colour-Rail*

CLASS 125
Built by British Railways, Derby Works

Right: These 1958/1959 Derby triple sets for the Lea Valley line had the best power/weight ratio of all the first-generation DMUs, the 238hp engines allowing them to keep up with EMUs on the Hertford East/Bishops Stortford and Cheshunt routes, and to tackle the climb from Liverpool Street to Bethnal Green. The orange star control equipment was drastically different from all other units, the throttle being fully pneumatically controlled rather than electro-pneumatically as in other units. This meant there was an extra air pipe on the bufferbeams to carry the throttle air between vehicles. There was therefore no wiring required to run through jumpers for throttle control and, being hydraulic transmission, there was no wiring required for the gears. The reduction in wiring meant that only one, albeit larger, jumper connection was required on either side, and this cable was fixed to the right of the bufferbeam.

Below: When the Lea Valley line was electrified, the '125s' moved to Finsbury Park to replace the Cravens units on services out of King's Cross. This move was short-lived, as the class was withdrawn by February 1977. No E51167 leads a set into the 'Cross' in November 1976. None survives. *Colour-Rail*

Numbers	Type	Class	Weight	Seats	Diagram	Lot No
E50988-51007	DMS	125/1	39 tons 10cwt	91	596	30462
E51154-51173	DMBS	125/2	39 tons 10cwt	65	595	30464
E59449-59468	TS	185	28 tons 10cwt	110	597	30463

CLASS 126
Built by British Railways, Swindon Works

The BTC desired trials of diesel units on fast city-to-city services, opting for the Scottish Region's premier line between Edinburgh and Glasgow. It was a short journey, just under 50 miles, and the fast turnaround of the sets could be used to full advantage. These first DMUs from Swindon were ordered just months after the first Derby cars, but it took them two years longer to provide the finished article. Services were introduced in January 1957 and some vehicles were also built for WR services between Birmingham and Cardiff and Swansea. However, this use was short-lived, as they were replaced by Swindon Cross-Country sets and were sent north

to join the rest of the fleet. Services were planned for three and six-car sets, the latter being two three-cars, only one of which would have a buffet. The gangwayed 'intermediate' power cars allowed access from the other set. However, for certain reasons, they were generally formed as leading power car, intermediate power car, two trailer cars (one buffet), intermediate power car, and leading power car. Normally, the intermediate power cars faced outwards, but the set pictured here at Haymarket Central Junction has the cab on the second vehicle facing inwards. Sideboards were carried on some cars and many of these sets never carried crests for the first few years. The front end design was very basic and was subject to much criticism. They lacked marker lights, destination and route blinds, simply having a changeable stencil stating the classification of the train (A, B or C; latterly 1, 2 or 3). *Colour-Rail*

Numbers	Type	Cab	Class	Seats	Weight	Diagram	Lot No	Year
Sc50936, 51008-51029	DMS (L)	Intermediate	126/1	64	39 tons 3cwt	551	30413	1959
Sc51030-51051	DMBS (L)	Leading	126/2	52	37 tons 16cwt	608	30414	1959
Sc59098-59099	TFRB (L)	-	187	18 & 12 buffet	34 tons 9cwt	560	30537	1961
Sc59391-59400	TF (L)	-	188	42	33 tons 8cwt	570	30415	1959
Sc59402-59412	TC (L)	-	189	18/32	31 tons 16cwt	571	30416	1959
W79083-79090	DMBS (L)	Intermediate	126/2	52	39 tons 13cwt	550	30196	1956
W79091-79094	DMBS (L)	Leading	126/2	52	38 tons 17cwt	552	30200	1956
Sc79095	DMBS (L)	Intermediate	126/2	52	39 tons 13cwt	550	30196	1956
Sc79096-79111	DMBS (L)	Leading	126/2	52	38 tons 17cwt	552	30200	1956
Sc79155-79168	DMS (L)	Intermediate	126/1	64	39 tons 3cwt	551	30199	1957
W79440-79441	TFRB (L)	-	187	18 & 12 buffet	34 tons 9cwt	560	30197	1957
Sc79442-79447	TFRB (L)	-	187	18 & 12 buffet	34 tons 9cwt	560	30197	1957
W79470-79473	TF(L)	-	188	42	33 tons 8cwt	570	30198	1956
Sc79474-79482	TF(L)	-	188	42	33 tons 8cwt	570	30198	1956

Above: The ScR requested further Inter-City sets for Ayrshire services, these being introduced in 1959 from Glasgow to Ayr, Girvan and Stranraer. To the same white circle coupling code, the underframe layout was redesigned from the 79xxx cars and the guard's vans were moved to the rear of the vehicles. A four-digit route indicator was added to the front, this being tastefully done, unlike on some classes. Intermediate power cars were again built, allowing through access between sets when correctly formed. A six-car set is seen heading north at Stevenston on 22 June 1962. Leading cars in this batch had jumper connections, but there does not seem to be any sign of the coupling codes painted on the cab. The jumper connections were painted white in the inner pair and black on the outer pair, the reverse of blue square cars. There were no inter-vehicle air pipes. *Colour-Rail*

Below: Here is an example of a three-car 79xxx series working. Now with a small yellow panel, the set has been repainted in the darker green, but still without any crests. The leading cars in this series lacked jumper connections, which no doubt led to operating problems. All power cars had 150hp engines. *G. M. Staddon*

Top: The application of the yellow panel to the intermediate power cars was not as neat as on other types that opted for a yellow gangway cover. This is not helped by the very neglected look of the vehicles. It was not always possible to connect an intermediate vehicle to another intermediate vehicle, while nine-car formations were not unusual. The second vehicle of this set, which is heading south at Newton-on-Ayr, is a buffet car, with a white window on the staff door. *D. A. Hope/Colour-Rail*

Above: There were two types of 79xxx series intermediate power car, one with a van and one without. A van version is taking the place of a leading car in this formation, and these could also be identified by the lack of water filler pipes on the cab front. The second vehicle lacks the van, and the layout of this car was identical to the Ayrshire DMS vehicles. The toilet on these was between the cab and the first vestibule and so had the filler pipes on the cab ends. The sets were replaced on the Edinburgh and Glasgow line in 1971 by

locomotive push-pull sets. It may appear to have been a very short lifespan, but it should not be reflected on the vehicles. The route involved intensive diagrams with high-speed running and an arduous climb from Glasgow Queen Street up Cowlairs incline, and the 14 years that these sets managed to operate the line has yet to be bettered by any traction that has followed! Some buffets were preserved, five power cars were exported to Liberia for use on a mining railway while a few joined the '126s' at Ayr depot. *G. M. Staddon*

Below: The sets were never refurbished, their non-standard status resulting in an early withdrawal. Their final months saw more diverse workings, including Glasgow to Carlisle via the G&SW route. The final modification was the removal of the gangways from the intermediate cars, the lower part of the rubbing plate being left, sometimes with the lamp brackets, as seen here on No Sc51017. Final withdrawals were in 1983, and a three-car set has been preserved. *Andrew McConnell*

CLASS 127
Built by British Railways, Derby Works

Numbers	Type	Class	Seating	Weight	Diagram	Lot No
M51591-51650	DMBS	127	78 (76)	40 tons	528	30521
M59589-59618	TS(L)	186	90	30 tons	589	30522
M59619-59648	TS	186	106	29 tons	590	30523

Above: Thirty of these Rolls-Royce 238hp powered quad sets were built at Derby in 1959 for services on the St Pancras to Bedford line, this earning them the name 'Bed-Pan' units. These were second-class only and were not gangwayed, but had a toilet for those that planned ahead and picked the right coach! The high-backed seating originally had 'winged' headrests and armrests on the ends, but these were found to restrict the number of passengers that could obtain a seat and were soon removed. They were the first DMU sets to be built with fluorescent lighting. The underframe equipment on this ex-works unit is painted in silver on at least the leading set of this formation, seen at Luton on 1 August 1959. After crew training, some sets were introduced the following month, but full timetable takeover was not until January 1960. *F. Hornby/Colour-Rail*

Above: Now with yellow panels, this set is seen on an up working at Hendon on 22 January 1963.

Above: The rear DMBS in this set has just a small yellow panel. This still carries the blue square coupling code. They were rebranded as red triangle sets in 1969, although no alterations were actually made to the control system. When coupled to a gearbox set these hydraulic sets had to be driven in a different manner to control the gearboxes in the remote cars.

After some serious incidents due to drivers not doing this, it was decided to discontinue the practice of running the two types together. The previous users of the red triangle code, the West Riding Derby Lightweight cars, had been withdrawn some years previously and would not have been compatible with the '127s'.

Left: The class was withdrawn from the route in 1983 after electrification. Centre cars were moved to Tyseley to allow asbestos-insulated Class 116 vehicles to be withdrawn. For this they were gangwayed and painted blue/grey for the first time. No M59596 was the first to be treated, in November 1983.
Malcolm Clements

CLASS 127

Top: Twenty-two of the power cars were converted to newspaper and express parcels vans. These were done in a variety of styles, initially without the roller shutter doors, which were fitted in different locations along the bodysides. Newspaper van No 55974 is seen at Barrow in September 1985. *Colour-Rail*

Above: In 1983, No 51591 was repainted in green livery and fitted with a plaque proclaiming that it was the first BR DMU to cover 1,250,000 miles. Still in passenger use, it initially worked in a set of blue vehicles on the Gospel Oak–Barking services. After withdrawal it was destined for the National Railway Museum, but was required to

be converted to a parcels car, becoming No M55966. This view shows it at Barrow in June 1986, paired with a vehicle that was painted green to match, while other '127s' in the blue/red stripe livery can be seen behind. The '127s' were withdrawn by 1989 with ten vehicles of the class preserved. *Colour-Rail*

Numbers	Weight	Diagram	Lot No
M55987-55990	40 tons	644	30552
W55991-55996	41 tons	643	30551

Above: The GWR had built some parcels railcars that proved very useful, so two designs were ordered from contractors by British Railways with those built by GRCW in 1960 being for the Western and London Midland Regions. The WR wanted gangways on them whereas the LMR did not. They were fitted with 230hp Albion engines, allowing them to take a 64-ton tail load. No M55990 is seen with two vans in tow on 25 April 1962. *Colour-Rail*

Left: As with the 1963 Inter-City sets, the application of yellow panels was done by having a yellow gangway cover. Previously, as the gangwayed sets had split headcode boxes and no space for whiskers, these had been painted on the gangway cover. With three ventilated vans and a CCT behind it, a car is seen at Iver in August 1964. *J. A. C. Kirke/Colour-Rail*

Above right: No 55991 is seen at Reading, now in blue, on 30 September 1985. By this date, only five of the ten remained: two at Reading, two at Newton Heath, and one at Chester. *Colour-Rail*

Right: No 55994 moved to Tyseley in late 1985 and was soon repainted in a two-tone blue livery with a red band. Its gangway is now gone, but the obsolete split boxes remain. No 55993 also appeared in these colours, but with some minor differences. *Colour-Rail*

Cravens built three 150hp AEC-engined parcels vans in 1958 with the yellow diamond coupling code to work with Derby Lightweights in the West Cumberland and Manchester areas. Delivered with whiskers, No M55998 displays a yellow panel when seen at Rugby on 4 April 1965. The vehicle has three filling positions on the side, the two lower ones for the fuel tank and the higher one for coolant. As with the passenger vehicles, the exhaust pipes passed up through the interior at the guard's compartment end and emitted through the roof. The inward-opening door identifies the guard's compartment, being shorter at the bottom. Note the crest is not centrally located the amount of small text on both ends of the bodywork! They ended their days working from Chester, and were withdrawn in 1972/73. One saw further use with the Railway Technical Centre, becoming 'Hydra' and used for hydraulic transmission and brake tests. None survives. *Colour-Rail*

Numbers	Weight	Diagram	Lot No
M55997-55999	30 tons	531	30418

Flavors of Rome

Flavors of Italy

Carla Bardi

Rome

and the Provinces
of Lazio

MᶜRAE BOOKS

ISBN 88-89272-04-X

This book was conceived, edited and designed by
McRae Books Srl, Borgo S. Croce 8, 50122, Florence, Italy
info@mcraebooks.com

Text: Carla Bardi
Photography: Marco Lanza
Home Economist: Rosalba Gioffrè
Design: Marco Nardi
Layouts: Ornella Fassio, Adriano Nardi, Adina Stefania Dragomir, Sara Mathews
Translation from the Italian: Linda Clearwater
Editing: Alison Leach, Anne McRae, Helen Farrell

2 4 6 8 10 9 7 5 3

Color separations: Fotolito Toscana, Florence, Italy
Printed and bound in Italy by D'Auria Industrie Grafiche Spa

Contents

Introduction

Lazio lies in the heart of Italy, midway between Tuscany in the north and Campania in the south. Despite its position, its inhabitants have rather more in common with the fun-loving peoples of the south than the rather terse, businesslike Tuscans to the north. The abundant Roman table reflects its peoples' temperament, and the business of eating in the Eternal City has been pursued with zeal and a delight in the spectacular since the times of the Roman Empire.

We have all heard of Roman banquets where course upon course of flamboyantly absurd dishes were served, from fattened dormice, to sweet and sour peaches, and the tongues of flamingoes and nightingales, all bathed in rancid fish sauces heavily flavored with spices. Many of these far-fetched dishes probably come from Petronius's comic novel *Satyricon*, the most famous episode of which mocks the immensely rich but vulgar Trimalchio and the banquet he gave to impress friends and hangers-on in Nero's decadent Rome. The reality of day-to-day eating habits in ancient Rome was far more sober: breakfast was a hearty meal, consisting at least in part of leftovers from the previous evening (cheese, bread, honey, eggs, and olives). Lunch was typically a light snack, taken in a city tavern or bought from any of the many street vendors. The main meal of the day was eaten at home in the evening, after a visit to the baths. A Roman dinner could start with a hearty soup made from cereals or legumes, or a platter of fresh vegetables. This might be followed by cheese, bread, milk, capers, and olives, with dried or fresh fruit to finish. Wealthier Romans might also have fish and, occasionally, meat. As Rome rose to its height and a few people became very rich, sumptuous evening banquets did become a part of the social and business scene. (For more information on food in ancient Rome see pages 66–67.)

The earliest Roman cookbook, called *De Arte Coquinaria*, was left to us by Marcus Gavius Apicius who lived in the 1st century AD. Anecdotes abound about this extravagant fellow, who reputedly squandered a fortune and then poisoned himself rather than live in poverty.

Left: lamb, cheese, bread, vegetables, and wine — staples of a Roman kitchen.

Below: the Colosseum, symbol of Rome.

One of Italy's best known wine stories comes from Montefiascone, on the shores of Lake Bolsena in northern Lazio. There are many versions, but according to most it was a prelate from Augsburg in Germany who, before setting out on a journey to Rome, sent a servant ahead of him to locate the inns with the best wines on the way. This would determine his itinerary. His servant was instructed to mark inns with good wine on a map with the word Est! Those serving excellent wine could merit Est! Est!! When the faithful servant reached the village of Montefiascone, he found the local wine so good that he marked it as Est! Est!! Est!!! And so it remains to the present day.

During the 5th century the Roman Empire finally collapsed under mounting pressure from invading Germanic and Slav peoples from the north and east. Rome itself was sacked several times and the last emperor, Augustulus, was deposed in 476. The long medieval period was marked by food shortages and famine, and it was the poorer classes who suffered most.

An amusing insight into dining in this period has been left to us in a little book of table manners called the *Piccolo Galateo Conviviale del Medioevo*. Directed at the upper classes, its suggestions for good table manners include: not asking what's on the menu, not eating things from other peoples' plates, not spitting food out, not drinking too much, and remembering to say grace before the meal begins. Table manners must certainly have deteriorated after this, because another *galateo*, published in the 16th century, instructed would-be refined diners "not to scratch themselves at the table; to avoid spitting except when strictly necessary, in which case to do it elegantly (!); not to stuff too much food into one's mouth at a time since this could lead to hiccoughs or other unseemly noises; not to clean one's teeth with the tablecloth; not to rinse one's mouth out with wine and then spit it out; and not to place one's toothpick behind one's ear, as a barber might."

The power vacuum left by the end of imperial rule was gradually filled by the papacy. By the 14th century, when the papacy was reunited in Rome (after a period of double papacy, split between Avignon in Provence and Rome), the papal court won renown for the brilliance of its banquets, at which elaborate foods and excellent wines were served. The growth in power of the papacy in Renaissance times was reflected in ever more splendid courtly banquets and, in particular, a real and detailed appreciation of the local wines.

However, it was only from the 16th century onward, with the arrival of products from the Americas, that the basis of Rome's present-day cooking tradition developed. The gradual introduction of tomatoes,

Dining in style with a view over the Eternal City.

potatoes, bell peppers (capsicums), eggplants (aubergines), corn, chocolate, sunflowers, turkey, and many other items changed the way people ate. Recipe books were written to help cooks to assimilate the new foods: the first book to explain corn and its uses, written by Virgilio Polidoro, was published in Rome in 1576.

Prosciutto and salami.

Writers, artists, and travelers of every nation flocked to Rome on their Grand Tours in the 18th and 19th centuries. Many have left us detailed records of every aspect of the city's food and wine. Veteran English traveler Mariana Starke even made a minute list of the price of foodstuffs! Gogol, Berlioz, Stendhal, Goethe, Thorvaldson, and a multitude of others passed through the city: by their notes we learn that pasta was already an important component of any menu, that *Fritto Misto* (see recipe, page 76) was frequently served, and that the local cheeses – ricotta, pecorino, and mozzarella – were equally delicious then as they are today. The local wines were obviously imbibed by all, since everyone appears to have something to say about them, for better or for worse. In general, the travelers approved of the Roman table, reserving special praise for the local fruit and vegetables.

Rome today: although Lazio is a fairly large and populous region, three of its five million inhabitants live in the city of Rome. The others are scattered among 370 communes in the other four provinces. Rome, the capital of Italy, contains within its historical center the tiny but powerful state of the Vatican City, headquarters of the Roman Catholic Church. Rome is a cosmopolitan city, bustling with bureaucrats, government officials, and religious officials and pilgrims from every part of Italy and the world. Like all large cities, Roman restaurants offer a wide variety of excellent foods from every region of Italy and from other countries. Nonetheless, traditional Roman fare is still to be found, particularly away from the tourist spots. Remember too, that, unlike Florence or Venice whose local characters have in many ways been overwhelmed by mass tourism, Rome has a large enough local population to have kept its unique, fun-loving character and cuisine. A small deviation down any side street or a trip outside the city center will bring you to a trattoria or osteria filled with locals enjoying the things they do best: eating and talking.

Romans don't do all their shopping in supermarkets and the city abounds in tiny cheese, cured meat, and vegetable shops, their wares often sprawling out the door onto the street.

A traditional Roman meal will begin with *Bruschetta* (see recipe, page 15), *Fave con pecorino* (see recipe, page 19), or *Carciofini sott'olio* (see recipe, page 18). This will be followed by a hearty and abundant first course, usually based on pasta. *Bucatini all'amatriciana* (see recipe, page 29) and *Spaghetti alla carbonara* (see recipe, page 32) are two you will find on every menu. Lamb is the most typical meat dish, prepared by roasting (*Abbacchio al forno*; see recipe, page 65) or braising (*Abbacchio alla romana*; see recipe, page 72). Side dishes will invariably include artichokes (*Carciofi alla giudia*; see recipe, page 86) and peas (*Piselli alla romana*; see recipe, page 85). If you can face it, the waiters will then offer you a choice from at least six homemade desserts from all over Italy. You will finish with an espresso and strong need for a siesta!

Rome's climate is highly conducive to outdoor dining, and cafés and trattorias flourish in the city from April until November. Dining on a sidewalk or tiny piazza on a hot summer night in Rome is one of life's great pleasures.

Fiumicino is an 18th-century fishing village on the outskirts of Rome. Fresh seafood is sold at the fish market along the port. Near the international airport, it is also a good, if crowded, place to take a swim in summer.

The castle of Tecchiena near the town of Alatri in Frosinone. The town itself, with its 4th-century BC walls and acropolis, is well worth a visit. A drive through the surrounding countryside, stopping off at a local trattoria for lunch, is a delightful way to spend a summer's day.

Rome now sprawls across an area much larger even than it did in imperial times when the Romans ruled half the known world, from Palestine to England. It has encompassed the coastal towns of Ostia (the port of ancient Rome) and Fiumicino. Both make pleasant day trips away from the bustle and heat of the central city. On the other side of town lies Tivoli, which hosts the still-imposing ruins of the Emperor Hadrian's Villa and the wonderfully refreshing 16th-century Villa d'Este. The gardens are full of fountains and water spraying, running, and dribbling in all directions, while the sumptuous villa itself gives us some idea of the splendor the popes allowed themselves.

Although the outlying provinces are relatively small compared to Rome, they all offer their own special produce, dishes, and wines. Beginning in the southeast: Frosinone is the capital of the area known as the Ciociaria. Inhabited by the ancient Volsci people from around 600 BC, the town was conquered by Rome as it expanded during the 4th century BC. Nowadays the province is devoted to agriculture and light industry. Excellent prosciutto, salami, pecorino, lamb, peas, strawberries, olives, and olive oil are typical local produce. Our recipe for *Frittata alla Ciociara* (see recipe, page 80) comes from this area. Wine has been made here for at least 20 centuries; the first recorded description was made by Pliny the Elder. Originally sweet and bubbly, today's Cesenese wines are mainly dry. The monks at the beautiful Cistercian monastery of Trisulti at Collepardo produce some delicious herbal liqueurs.

Latina is the capital of this southern province, most of which was covered in inhospitable marshland from the Middle Ages until the 1940s, when it was successfully drained. The reclaimed land of the Pontine plains is now dedicated to market gardening, farming, and industry. Tomatoes, artichokes and other vegetables, cheese, and lamb are produced here.

The many ancient towns along the coast serve some excellent seafood. The wonderful sweet and sour dish *Tiella con Pesce* (see recipe, page 47) comes from Gaeta in the south. The cooking in this area has much in common with the nearby city of Naples. The local wines, from Cori, Aprilia, and the south, were not widely known outside the area until recently. In the last ten years or so, some have been exported, even as far afield as North America. Most are simple dry or medium whites and reds, which team up beautifully with the local foods.

The northern province of Viterbo is home to many ancient Etruscan towns: Tuscania, Viterbo, Tarquinia, and Cerveteri were all important centers of Etruscan culture. This is also the province of Lake Bolsena, the largest lake in Italy. Local dishes include many based on eels and trout from the lake. Some of Lazio's best wines are produced along the shores of the lake. The area is also known for its cherries, strawberries, pears, figs, and other fruits. Farther south, the area around Lake Bracciano produces some of the region's best cured meats. Fish and seafood are popular along the coast. The coastal town of Civitavecchia is also the hometown of a rather complicated but delicious traditional cake – *Pizza Dolce Civitavecchiese* (see recipe, page 106). Gastronomically Viterbo is a varied province, sharing many dishes and traditions with Rome, but also with Tuscany and Umbria.

The inland province of Rieti came to Lazio from Umbria and its gastronomy reflects its historical ties. It also has strong ties with neighboring Abruzzo. However, we shouldn't forget that this is the zone which gave Rome one of its most famous dishes – *Bucatini all'Amatriciana* (see recipe, page 29). The dish is named for the town of Amatrice in the extreme northeast of the province. This area also produces good lamb, kid, ricotta, pecorino, and cured meats. Black truffles are also found here in the fall.

Fountain in the courtyard of the 13th-century Papal Palace at Viterbo. The city has a beautiful medieval center which, although badly damaged during World War II, has been carefully restored.

The deserted coastlines of Latina are great places to get away from it all, either on foot or horseback.

Antipasti

Roman cooking is essentially simple and rustic and the few typical appetizers reflect this tradition. A special meal could begin with a platter of locally cured meats, olives, pickled vegetables, and a selection of crostini. Toasted bread with garlic and oil is the most classic crostino. These dishes are all rooted in the region's peasant origins—the above list could be a typical plowman's lunch of a century ago. Other elaborate classics include pancakes with pecorino or meat sauce and Fried mozzarella sandwiches.

Bruschetta

Toasted bread with garlic and oil

Toast the bread until golden brown on both sides. ▪ Rub half a garlic clove evenly over each slice. The crisp toast works like a grater. Drizzle with the oil and season with salt and pepper to taste. Serve hot.

Serves: 4
Preparation: 5 minutes
Cooking: 5 minutes
Recipe grading: easy

- 4–8 slices day-old, firm-textured bread
- 2–4 cloves garlic, peeled
- 4–8 tablespoons high-quality extra-virgin olive oil
- salt and freshly ground black pepper

Suggested wine: a dry white
(Frascati Secco)

Bruschetta *is a common appetizer throughout central Italy, but the Romans claim to have invented it. For a successful dish you must use only the freshest and best quality extra-virgin olive oil. Choose a dark green, translucent oil from a good specialty store. Be sure to check the expiry date on the bottle; even the best olive oil keeps only for about a year. Never buy oil that doesn't carry a production or expiry date.*

Serves: 4
Preparation: 20 minutes
Cooking: about 1 hour
Recipe grading: fairly easy

- 2 tablespoons dried porcini mushrooms
- 2 cups/500 ml cold water
- 5 large, very ripe tomatoes, peeled
- ½ cup/125 g butter, chopped
- salt
- 1¾ cups/350 g rice (Italian semifino or fino)
- ½ cup/60 g freshly grated parmesan cheese
- 2 large eggs
- 1 small onion, finely chopped
- 1 stalk celery, finely chopped
- 1¼ cups/150 g ground/minced beef
- 4 chicken livers, finely chopped
- ½ cup/60 g finely chopped prosciutto/ Parma ham
- 3½ oz/100 g mozzarella cheese, diced in ½ inch/1-cm cubes
- scant 2 cups/100 g fresh bread crumbs
- 1–2 cups/250–500 ml olive oil, for frying

Suggested wine: a dry white
(Frascati Superiore)

Supplì alla romana

Filled rice balls

Place the mushrooms in a small bowl and cover with warm water. Leave to soften for about 20 minutes. ▪ Put the cold water, 4 chopped tomatoes, three-quarters of the butter, and salt in a large saucepan. Bring to a boil and add the rice. Stir frequently and cook until the rice is ready. ▪ Remove from the heat and stir in the parmesan and the eggs. Spread the mixture out on a large plate to cool. ▪ In the meantime, drain the mushrooms and chop coarsely. Heat the remaining butter in a small skillet (frying pan) and sauté the mushrooms with the onion, celery, beef, chicken livers, and prosciutto for 4–5 minutes over a medium heat. ▪ Add the remaining chopped tomato and season with salt. Cover and cook over a low heat for about 20 minutes, or until the sauce has reduced. Stir frequently so that the sauce doesn't stick. ▪ Use a tablespoon to scoop up some rice and shape it into a ball about the size of an egg. Make a hollow in the ball of rice and fill with the meat sauce and one or two cubes of cheese. Seal with a little more rice. Roll the filled rice ball in the bread crumbs and set it aside on a plate. Repeat until all the rice, meat sauce, and cheese have been used. ▪ Heat the oil in a large skillet pan until very hot, but not smoking. Fry the rice balls until crisp and golden brown all over. ▪ Drain on paper towels and serve immediately.

For a lighter dish, fry the rice balls in batches of 5–6. The temperature of the oil should not drop too much when you add the rice balls. This stops them from absorbing too much oil. Supplì make a very hearty appetizer; you may prefer to serve it as a first course or even as a main course with a salad.

Serves: 4
Preparation: 20 minutes + 2 months'
preserving
Cooking: 10 minutes
Recipe grading: easy

- 8–12 fresh globe artichokes
- juice of 1 lemon
- 2 quarts/2 liters cold water
- 8 tablespoons white wine vinegar
- salt
- extra-virgin olive oil

Suggested wine: a light, dry white
(Colli Albani Secco)

Carciofini sott'olio

Artichokes preserved in oil

Clean the artichokes by trimming the tops and stalks. Remove all the tough outer leaves so that only the pale, tender hearts remain. Place in a bowl of cold water with the lemon juice for 15 minutes. • Bring the water, vinegar, and salt to a boil in a large saucepan. Drain the artichokes and add to the saucepan. Cook for 10 minutes. • Drain the artichokes and dry well with paper towels. Transfer to clean preserving jars and cover with oil. Seal the jars and set aside in a cool, dark place for at least 2 months before serving.

Delicious served on their own, these tasty little hearts are also good with a platter or sliced, cured meats (salami, ham, prosciutto).

Fave con pecorino

Fava beans with ewe's cheese

Rinse the beans thoroughly under cold running water. Dry well on a clean dishcloth. Discard any tough or withered-looking pods, or any with ugly spots or marks. Place in an attractive serving dish. ▪ Serve with the cheese already cut into dice, or in a wedge cut from the round.

Serves: 6–8
Preparation: 5 minutes
Recipe grading: easy

- 4 lb/2 kg fresh, young fava beans/ broad beans in their pods
- 8½–12 oz/250–350 g pecorino romana ewe's cheese

Suggested wine: a dry, aromatic white (Bianco Capena)

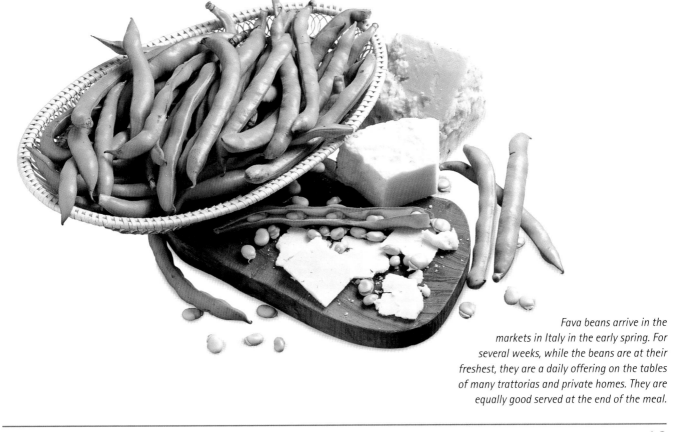

Fava beans arrive in the markets in Italy in the early spring. For several weeks, while the beans are at their freshest, they are a daily offering on the tables of many trattorias and private homes. They are equally good served at the end of the meal.

Serves: 4
Preparation: 10 minutes + 1 hour's resting
Cooking: 15 minutes
Recipe grading: fairly easy

- 4 large, thin slices firm-textured bread
- freshly ground black pepper
- 12 oz/350 g mozzarella cheese, sliced
- 4 anchovy fillets, crumbled (optional)
- scant 1 cup/200 ml milk
- ¾ cup/125 g all-purpose/plain flour
- 2 large eggs
- dash of salt
- 1–2 cups/250–500 ml olive oil, for frying

Suggested wine: a dry white (Orvieto)

Pandorato ripieno

Fried mozzarella sandwiches

Remove the crusts from the bread and cut each slice in halves or quarters. Season with pepper. ▪ Cover half the bread with the mozzarella slices and the anchovies, if using. Place the remaining slices of bread over the top to make little sandwiches. ▪ Dip the sandwiches briefly into the milk, then sprinkle well with flour. Arrange the sandwiches on a large plate. ▪ Beat the eggs with the salt and pour over the sandwiches. Leave for about 1 hour so that the egg is completely absorbed. ▪ Heat the oil in a large skillet (frying pan) until very hot, but not smoking. Fry the sandwiches a few at a time until they are deep golden brown all over. ▪ Drain well and place on paper towels. ▪ Serve hot.

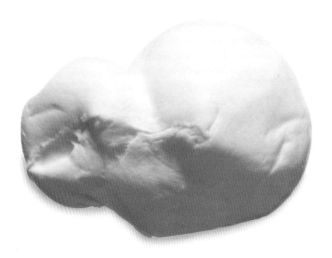

*This hearty appetizer also makes
a nourishing snack or light lunch.*

The wines of Lazio

Lazio can probably boast the longest unbroken wine-making tradition in the world. The Etruscans, who inhabited the area 800 years BC, were already experienced vintners. The Romans inherited their traditions and huge quantities of locally grown wine were consumed in the halcyon days of the empire. Served with water, it was the most common drink and appeared on the table at all mealtimes. During the Renaissance, the popes maintained a lively interest in wine, both local and imported. Today Lazio is known for its white wines, most of which are produced in the Alban Hills and Aprilia near Rome. To the north, around the beautiful Lake Bolsena, some excellent whites are also produced. To the west, on the coast at Cerveteri, some of the region's best reds are made.

The Alban hills encircle the city of Rome on three sides. It is here, in the six DOC zones, that most of Lazio's white wines are made. The northern hills are known as the Castelli Romani, and the central and southern parts as the Colli Albani. Frascati, Colli Albani, Velletri, and Zagarolo are the best-known wines from here. To the north, Est! Est!! Est!!! di Montefiascone, was named by a papal envoy sent to test the local wines and told to code the best as Est! This one was so good that it merited three!

In days of old, the wines from the Alban Hills were brought into Rome by horse and cart. Stories abound of the mischief and fun the journey involved, and Roman cuisine even has recipes dedicated to these loyal workers.

The best reds in Lazio are produced in the coastal region of Cerveteri. The Ciociaria area, east of the Alban Hills, is also best known for its reds.

Lazio makes its share of *spumante* and sweet dessert wines. *Aleatico di Gradoli*, similar to port, is the oldest of the sweet wines. The whole area has responded to the increasing demand for light sparkling wines by producing dozens of them.

The Castelli Romani zone takes its name from the beautiful castles that dot the hillsides. Many are owned by winegrowers and operate as cellars. This is the Villa Aldobrandini at Frascati.

Serves: 4–6
Preparation: 5 minutes
Cooking: 25 minutes
Recipe grading: easy

- 3 large eggs
- salt
- 1 cup/150 g all-purpose/plain white flour
- scant ½ cup/100 ml warm milk
- 3–4 tablespoons butter or extra-virgin olive oil
- 1 cup/125 g freshly grated pecorino romano cheese

Suggested wine: a dry white (Orvieto)

Pizzacce

Pancakes with ewe's cheese

Beat the eggs with the salt. ▪ Stir in the flour, then add the milk and stir to obtain a smooth batter. It should be about the consistency of pancake batter. If necessary, add more milk or flour to obtain the right consistency. ▪ Heat the butter or oil in a small skillet (frying pan) until very hot. Add 1–2 tablespoons of batter and twirl the pan so that it spreads evenly across the bottom. Cook until brown, then toss to brown the other side. Repeat until all the batter is used up. ▪ Sprinkle the fritters with pecorino and serve hot.

This Roman version of savory pancakes is a favorite with children and adults alike.

Pizzacce di Rieti

Baked pancakes with meat sauce

Prepare the meat sauce. ▪ Prepare the Pizzacce. ▪ Roll the pancakes loosely and arrange them in an ovenproof baking dish. Spoon the sauce over the top and sprinkle with the pecorino. Season with cayenne or chile pepper, if liked. ▪ Bake in a preheated oven at 400°F/200°C/gas 6 for 10 minutes, or until the cheese is light, golden brown. ▪ Serve hot.

Serves: 4–6
Preparation: 5 minutes + time to make the meat sauce and pancakes
Cooking: about 10 minutes
Recipe grading: easy

▪ 1 quantity Meat sauce (choose from: sausage sauce on page 34, the mushroom and liver sauce on page 38, or the clove-flavored meat sauce on page 48)

▪ 1 quantity Pizzacce – see recipe, facing page

▪ 1¼ cups/150 g freshly grated pecorino romano cheese

▪ dash of cayenne or chile pepper (optional)

Suggested wine: a dry red
(Velletri Rosso Secco)

These pancakes make a warming winter appetizer. They are quite filling so you won't need to serve a first course afterward.

Fiori di zucca farciti

Stuffed fried zucchini flowers

Serves: 4
Preparation: 10 minutes
Cooking: 15 minutes
Recipe grading: fairly easy

- 20 fresh zucchini/courgette flowers
- 6 anchovy fillets, crumbled
- 1 cup/125 g fine bread crumbs
- 1 tablespoon finely chopped parsley
- 3 large eggs
- salt and freshly ground black pepper
- 2/3 cup/100 g all-purpose/plain flour
- 1–2 cups/250–500 ml olive oil, for frying

Suggested wine: a dry, fruity white
(Colli Albani Secco)

Rinse the flowers carefully under cold running water. Trim the stalks and dry the flowers carefully with paper towels. ▪ Mix the anchovies with the bread crumbs in a bowl. Add the parsley, 1 egg, and salt and pepper (since the anchovies are already salty, you may not need much salt). Mix well. ▪ Use this mixture to carefully stuff the flowers. ▪ Beat the remaining eggs and place them in a shallow bowl. Place the flour in a shallow bowl and dip the stuffed flowers first in the flour, then in the egg. ▪ Heat the oil in a large skillet (frying pan) until very hot, but not smoking. Fry the flowers in batches of 5–6 at a time. Turn them so that they brown all over. ▪ Drain on paper towels. Repeat until all the flowers are cooked. Sprinkle with a little salt, if liked. ▪ Serve hot.

The anchovies give this recipe a little extra zing. However, if you don't like them you may leave them out. The dish will be a little blander, but delicious all the same.

Primi piatti

Rome has a wide variety of pasta dishes and first courses of all kinds. This is the home of a thick type of spaghetti with a hollowed-out middle called "bucatini". They are served most often all'Amatriciana, which is a spicy tomato sauce named for a town in the hills above the city (see next page). Other pasta favorites include alla Carbonara with an egg and bacon sauce, and the very simple garlic and oil, or pecorino cheese and pepper sauces. There are also many soups made with vegetables or eggs, plus two types of gnocchi.

Bucatini all'amatriciana

Bucatini with tomato and pancetta

Place a large pot of cold water over a high heat. ▪ Sauté the pancetta in the oil for 2–3 minutes. ▪ Add the chile pepper and onion, if using, and sauté for 2–3 minutes more. ▪ Pour in the wine and cook for 2–3 minutes until the wine evaporates. Season with salt and pepper. ▪ Peel the tomatoes and dice them. Add to the pan and cook over a medium heat for about 15 minutes, or until the tomatoes have reduced. ▪ When the water in the pot is boiling, add the coarse sea salt, then the bucatini and cook for the time indicated on the package. ▪ Drain the pasta when it is cooked al dente and transfer to a large heated serving dish. Pour the sauce over the top and sprinkle with the cheese. Toss well and serve.

Serves: 4
Preparation: 10 minutes
Cooking: 25 minutes
Recipe grading: easy

- 1¼ cups/150 g diced pancetta
- 2 tablespoons extra-virgin olive oil
- ¼ teaspoon crushed chile pepper
- 1 onion (optional)
- 4 tablespoons dry white wine
- salt and freshly ground black pepper
- 1 lb/500 g ripe tomatoes
- 2 tablespoons coarse sea salt
- 1 lb/500 g bucatini pasta
- 4 tablespoons freshly grated pecorino cheese

Suggested wine: a dry white (Frascati Secco)

This recipe takes its name from Amatrice, a lovely town in the hills of the province of Rieti.

Spaghetti alla puttanesca

Spaghetti with black olives

Place a large pot of cold water over a high heat. ▪ Peel the tomatoes and dice them. Pit (stone) and chop about three-quarters of the olives. ▪ Heat the oil in a skillet (frying pan) and sauté the garlic with the chile pepper. Discard the garlic when it has turned light gold. Add the anchovies (if using) and stir well in the oil until they dissolve. ▪ Add the olives and capers, then the tomatoes. Season with salt and pepper (the anchovies and olives are both quite salty, so be sure to taste the sauce before seasoning). Cook over a medium-low heat for about 15 minutes, or until the sauce reduces. ▪ When the water in the pot is boiling, add the coarse sea salt, then the spaghetti and cook for the time indicated on the package. ▪ Drain the pasta when it is cooked al dente and transfer to a large heated serving dish. Pour the sauce over the top, toss well, and serve.

Serves: 4
Preparation: 10 minutes
Cooking: 25 minutes
Recipe grading: easy

- 1 lb/500 g ripe tomatoes
- 8 oz/250 g black olives
- 2 tablespoons extra-virgin olive oil
- 2 cloves garlic, peeled and whole
- ½ teaspoon crushed chile pepper
- 4 anchovy fillets (optional)
- 2 tablespoons capers
- salt and freshly ground black pepper
- 2 tablespoons coarse sea salt
- 1 lb/500 g spaghetti

Suggested wine: a dry white
(Castelli Romani)

This fiery dish is named after the not very polite Italian word "puttana", which refers to women practicing the oldest profession in the world. The anchovies are not optional in the classic recipe, although since many people don't like their taste, they can be left out.

Spaghetti alla carbonara
Spaghetti with egg and bacon sauce

Serves: 4
Preparation: 10 minutes
Cooking: about 15 minutes
Recipe grading: easy

- 1¼ cups/150 g diced smoked pancetta or bacon
- 1 tablespoon extra-virgin olive oil
- 1 clove garlic, lightly crushed but whole
- 2 tablespoons coarse sea salt
- 1 lb/500 g spaghetti
- 5 large eggs
- 3½ tablespoons light/single cream (optional)
- salt and freshly ground black pepper
- 4 tablespoons each freshly grated parmesan and pecorino cheese

Suggested wine: a light, dry rosé
(Castelli Romani Rosato)

Place a large pot of cold water over a high heat. ▪ Sauté the pancetta or bacon in the oil with the garlic. Discard the garlic when it has turned pale gold. ▪ When the water in the pot is boiling, add the coarse sea salt, then the spaghetti and cook for the time indicated on the package. ▪ While the spaghetti is cooking, beat the eggs with the cream (if using), a dash of salt, the cheeses, and a generous grinding of pepper in a large bowl. ▪ Drain the pasta very thoroughly when it is cooked al dente and transfer to the bowl with the egg mixture. ▪ Add the pasta to the pancetta and oil and toss vigorously over a low heat for 2 minutes. ▪ Serve at once.

This dish is said to have been invented during the last days of World War II. When US troops arrived in Rome, they brought an abundant supply of eggs and bacon which ingenious local cooks used to make the now classic Roman carbonara.

Spaghetti aglio e olio

Spaghetti with garlic and oil sauce

Place a large pot of cold water over a high heat. ▪ Heat the oil in a skillet (frying pan) and sauté the garlic until pale gold. ▪ When the water in the pot is boiling, add the coarse sea salt, then the spaghetti and cook for the time indicated on the package. ▪ Drain the pasta when it is cooked al dente and transfer to the skillet with the garlic and oil. Season with a generous grinding of pepper, if liked. Toss over a low heat for 1 minute. ▪ Serve hot.

Serves: 4
Preparation: 5 minutes
Cooking: about 15 minutes
Recipe grading: easy

- ▪ ½ cup/125 ml extra-virgin olive oil
- ▪ 3 cloves garlic, lightly crushed
- ▪ 2 tablespoons coarse sea salt
- ▪ 1 lb/500 g spaghetti
- ▪ freshly ground black pepper (optional)

Suggested wine: a dry, fruity white
(Colli Albani Secco)

Another classic dish has exactly the same ingredients as this one, with the addition of about ½ teaspoon of crushed chile peppers.

Serves: 6
Preparation: 10 minutes
Cooking: 50 minutes
Recipe grading: fairly easy

- 3 tablespoons lard (or butter)
- 1 onion, finely chopped
- 1 stalk celery, finely chopped
- 1 small carrot, finely chopped
- 2 tablespoons finely chopped flat-leaf parsley
- 1 tablespoon concentrated tomato paste dissolved in ½ cup/125 ml cold water
- salt
- 10 oz/300 g Italian sausage
- scant 3 quarts/2.75 liters cold water
- 1 tablespoon coarse sea salt
- 3¼ cups/500 g finely ground cornmeal/ polenta

Suggested wine: a young, full-bodied red (Sangiovese di Aprilia)

Polenta sulla spianatoia

Polenta with sausage sauce

Melt the lard in a skillet (frying pan) and sauté the onion, celery, carrot, and parsley over a medium heat until the vegetables have softened. ▪ Add the tomato paste and water, season with salt, then cover the skillet and cook over a medium-low heat for about 30 minutes. ▪ Peel the sausage and chop coarsely. Add to the vegetables and cook for 15 minutes more. ▪ Meanwhile prepare the polenta: bring the water to a boil with the sea salt. Gradually sprinkle in the cornmeal while stirring continuously with a large balloon whisk to stop lumps from forming. ▪ Cook over a low heat, stirring continuously for about 40 minutes. ▪ When cooked, turn out onto a polenta board (or large serving platter) and spoon the sauce over the top. ▪ Serve hot.

Polenta originally comes from northern Italy, but has now spread to every region. This recipe is popular in Lazio during the winter months.

Pecorino and ricotta cheese

Rome was founded by pastoralists during the 8th century BC, so cheese-making is one of the region's most ancient gastronomic traditions. Ancient Roman writers have left records of several cheeses, including those from Vestino, Trebula, and Luni, as well as a smoked variety from Velabrum (these are all areas of ancient Latium). Cheese was an

important source of protein during Classical times when meat was too expensive for most people. Ancient Roman cheeses were mostly made from the milk of sheep and goats. Many were served warm, perhaps after being cooked in the oven or over a grill. Cheeses

were also mixed with crushed wheat and water to make savory breads or flavored with herbs and garlic and spread over bread to make a sort of ancient focaccia.

Lazio is still an important cheese-producing region. Pecorino romano, made from ewes' milk, is probably the best known of the local cheeses and is a major export item. Fresh creamy ricotta, also made from ewes' milk, is the other local favorite, although a variety of different cheeses are also produced. Caciotta, caciottone, and provatura are three of the better known traditional cheeses. They are not well known outside Lazio itself.

Flocks of ewes thrive in among the olive groves that dot the landscape of Lazio. Their tasty milk is used to make both ricotta and pecorino cheese.

Forms of authentic pecorino romano bear a special brand (right) to show that they have been made within the designated area. This area now includes the provinces of Frosinone, Latina, Roma, and Viterbo, as well as parts of southern Tuscany and all of the island of Sardinia.

The art of making ricotta cheese was re-introduced to Lazio after the fall of the Roman Empire by Saint Francis of Assisi. While this cheese is made throughout Italy, the Roman variety is slightly drier and more compact than the ones produced in other regions.

Pecorino romano is a salty, aromatic cheese. Well-aged it makes an ideal grating cheese, while the younger varieties are served as table cheeses. The hefty forms – each one weighs about 50 lb (25 kg) – are produced from October through July each year and are aged for anywhere between four to twelve months.

Forms and containers of ricotta and pecorino cheese ready for eating or aging.

Serves: 4
Preparation: 20 minutes (if using homemade
   fettuccine + time to make it)
Cooking: 30 minutes
Recipe grading: easy

- 1 lb/500 g fresh homemade or store-
  bought fettuccine (to make the pasta
  see recipe, page 49)
- salt
- 4 tablespoons freshly grated
  pecorino cheese

For the sauce:
- 2 tablespoons dried porcini mushrooms
- 3 tablespoons coarsely chopped
  pork fat
- 1 small onion, finely chopped
- 1 clove garlic, finely chopped
- 1²/₃ cups/400 g fresh or canned peeled
  and chopped tomatoes
- salt and freshly ground black pepper
- 8 oz/250 g trimmed, diced chicken livers
- 6 tablespoons butter
- 4 tablespoons dry white wine
- ½ cup/125 ml broth (homemade or
  bouillon cube)

Suggested wine: a dry red (Sangiovese)

Fettuccine alla romana

Roman-style fettuccine

Prepare the fettuccine (if using homemade pasta). ▪ Place a large pot of cold, salted water over a high heat. ▪ Place the mushrooms in a small bowl of warm water and leave to soften for 15 minutes. ▪ Melt the pork fat in a skillet (frying pan) over a moderate heat and sauté the onion and garlic. ▪ Drain the mushrooms and add to the sauce together with the tomatoes. Season with salt and pepper. Cook over a moderate heat for about 15 minutes, or until the sauce reduces. ▪ Clean the chicken livers, cutting off and discarding any stringy membranes. Chop coarsely. ▪ Melt half the butter in a small, heavy-bottomed pan and cook the chicken livers over a moderate heat for 4–5 minutes. Pour in the wine and cook until it evaporates. ▪ Add the broth, then cover and cook over a low heat until the chicken livers are well-cooked (about 15 minutes). ▪ Add the chicken livers to the tomato sauce. ▪ When the water in the pot is boiling, add the fettuccine and cook for 3–5 minutes, if homemade (or the time indicated on the package, if store-bought). ▪ Drain the fettuccine and transfer to a heated serving bowl. Add the sauce and toss vigorously for 1–2 minutes. ▪ Sprinkle with the cheese and serve at once.

If preparing the pasta at home, the fettuccine
should be cut about ½ in/1 cm in width.

Serves: 4
Preparation: 5 minutes
Cooking: about 10 minutes
Recipe grading: easy

- 2 tablespoons coarse sea salt
- 1 lb/500 g spaghetti
- 1¼ cups/150 g freshly grated
  pecorino cheese
- freshly ground black pepper

Suggested wine: a young, dry red
(Frascati Novello)

Spaghetti cacio e pepe
Spaghetti with cheese and pepper

Place a large pot of cold water over a high heat. ▪ When the water is boiling, add the coarse sea salt, then the spaghetti and cook for the time indicated on the package. ▪ Drain the pasta when it is cooked al dente, leaving just a little more water than usual. This will help to melt the cheese and will prevent the pasta from sticking together. ▪ Transfer the spaghetti to a large heated serving dish. Sprinkle the pecorino over the top. Cover with a generous grinding of pepper and toss energetically for 1–2 minutes. ▪ Serve at once.

Spaghetti al tonno

Spaghetti with tuna and tomato

Serves: 4
Preparation: 10 minutes
Cooking: about 15 minutes
Recipe grading: easy

Place a large pot of cold water over a high heat. ▪ Sauté the garlic and parsley in the oil in a large skillet (frying pan) over a moderate heat for 3–4 minutes. ▪ Add the tomatoes, season with salt and pepper, and cook for 15 minutes, or until the sauce reduces. ▪ When the water in the pot is boiling, add the coarse sea salt, then the spaghetti, and cook for the time indicated on the package. ▪ Mix the tuna into the tomato sauce, stir well, then remove from the heat. ▪ Drain the pasta when it is cooked al dente and transfer to a large heated serving dish. Add the tomato and tuna sauce and toss vigorously for 1–2 minutes. ▪ Serve at once.

- 2 cloves garlic, finely chopped
- 2 tablespoons finely chopped flat-leaf parsley
- 4 tablespoons extra-virgin olive oil
- 6 large ripe tomatoes, peeled and diced
- salt and freshly ground black pepper
- 2 tablespoons coarse sea salt
- 1 lb/500 g spaghetti
- 8 oz/250 g tuna fish, packed in oil, drained, and flaked

Suggested wine: a dry white
(Vignanello Bianco Secco)

This sauce is easy to prepare and very tasty. It goes well with spaghetti, but perhaps even better with the smaller spaghettini.

Tagliatelle con prosciutto e piselli

Tagliatelle with prosciutto and peas

Prepare the tagliatelle (if using homemade pasta). ▪ Place a large pot of cold water over a high heat. ▪ Cook the peas in a small pot of lightly salted water until just cooked. Drain and set aside. ▪ Melt the butter in a skillet (frying pan) and sauté the onion and prosciutto for 5 minutes. ▪ Add the peas and season with salt and pepper. Leave to cook for 5 minutes. ▪ When the water is boiling, add the coarse sea salt, then the tagliatelle and cook for 5–7 minutes, or until cooked al dente. This depends on the type of tagliatelle used. Fresh tagliatelle takes a lot less time to cook than the dried store-bought type. ▪ Drain the tagliatelle and transfer to a heated serving dish. Sprinkle with the parmesan and serve at once.

Serves: 4
Preparation: 10 minutes (if using homemade tagliatelle + time to make it)
Cooking: about 20 minutes
Recipe grading: easy

- 1 lb/500 g fresh homemade or store-bought tagliatelle (to make the pasta see recipe, page 49)
- 2¼ cups/290 g fresh (shelled weight) or frozen peas
- salt and freshly ground black pepper
- 4 tablespoons butter
- 1 small onion, finely chopped
- 1 cup/120 g prosciutto, cut in one thick slice and diced
- 6 tablespoons freshly grated parmesan cheese
- 2 tablespoons coarse sea salt

Suggested wine: a dry white
(Est! Est!! Est!!!)

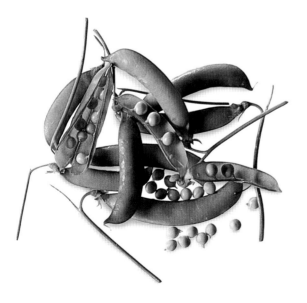

To make the pasta at home, follow the instructions on page 49. The tagliatelle should be cut about ¼ in/6 mm in width.

Serves: 4
Preparation: 15 minutes
Cooking: about 40 minutes
Recipe grading: fairly easy

- 10 oz/300 g chicken livers
- 6 tablespoons butter
- 1 medium onion, finely chopped
- 4 tablespoons dry white wine
- 2¼ cups/310 g peeled and diced fresh or canned tomatoes
- salt and freshly ground black pepper
- 2 cups/400 g rice
- 4¼ cups/1 liter meat broth (homemade or bouillon cube), boiling
- 4 tablespoons freshly grated parmesan cheese

Suggested wine: a dry red (Cerveteri Rosso)

Timballo del papa

Papal rice mold

Clean the chicken livers, cutting off and discarding any stringy membranes. Chop coarsely. ▪ Heat two-thirds of the butter in a deep-sided skillet (frying pan) and sauté the onion until pale gold. ▪ Add the chicken livers and stir until they are brown. ▪ Pour in the wine and cook until it has evaporated. ▪ Add the tomatoes and cook for 15 minutes, or until the sauce reduces. Season with salt and pepper. ▪ Add the rice and a little broth. Keep stirring and adding broth until the rice is cooked al dente. ▪ Remove the skillet from the heat and stir in the parmesan. ▪ Grease the sides of a ring mold with the remaining butter. Transfer the rice mixture to the mold and press down well. ▪ Bake in a preheated oven at 400°F/200°C/gas 6 for 10 minutes. ▪ Turn the baked mold out onto a heated platter and serve at once.

With the exception of one or two seafood dishes, risottos are not typical of Lazio and the few recipes featuring rice are usually soups. This rather elaborate Papal Rice Mold is reserved for very special occasions.

Tiella con pesce

Sweet and sour squid pie

Crumble the yeast into a small bowl and add the sugar and half the water, stirring until the yeast dissolves. ▪ Leave to stand for 10 minutes in a warm (not hot) place; the surface will become frothy. ▪ Sift the flour into a large mixing bowl with the salt. Make a well in the center and pour in the yeast liquid, the oil, and most of the remaining water. ▪ Stir with a wooden spoon until the flour has been absorbed. Add a little more warm water if necessary. ▪ Place the dough on a floured work surface and knead until it becomes very soft and elastic. ▪ Shape into a ball and place in a large bowl. Cover with a large clean cloth folded in half and leave to rise in a warm place, away from drafts, for 1 hour, or until the dough has doubled in volume. ▪ Knead the dough briefly on a lightly floured surface just before using. ▪ Heat the oil in a large skillet (frying pan) and sauté the garlic for 2–3 minutes. ▪ Remove the garlic and add the squid. Cook over a moderate heat, stirring frequently, for 15 minutes. ▪ Stir in the other ingredients and cook for 5 minutes. Season with salt and pepper. ▪ Divide the dough into two portions, one almost twice as large as the other. Roll the larger piece of dough out to a thickness of about ⅛ in/3 mm. Use it to line the bottom and sides of a springform pan (tin). Leave enough dough to slightly overlap the edges. ▪ Fill the dough-lined springform pan with the squid mixture. ▪ Roll out the smaller piece of dough to the same thickness as the first and use it to cover the springform pan. Fold the overlapping dough over the top to seal. ▪ Bake in a preheated oven at 400°F/200°C/gas 6 for 30 minutes. ▪ Serve hot or at room temperature.

Serves: 4
Preparation: 30 minutes + 1 hour's rising
Cooking: about 1 hour
Recipe grading: fairly easy

For the dough:

- ½ oz/15 g compressed/fresh baker's yeast or 1 tablespoon active dried yeast
- 1 teaspoon sugar
- about ¾ cup/180 ml warm water
- 2⅓ cups/350 g unbleached or all-purpose/strong plain flour, plus 2 tablespoons extra flour
- 1–2 teaspoons salt
- 2½ tablespoons extra-virgin olive oil

For the filling:

- 4 tablespoons extra-virgin olive oil
- 1 clove garlic
- 14 oz/400 g squid (cleaned and prepared weight-ask your fish vendor to prepare it), coarsely chopped
- 4 ripe tomatoes, peeled and diced
- 1½ cups/200 g pitted black olives
- 3 tablespoons golden raisins/sultanas
- 3 tablespoons pine nuts
- 3 tablespoons capers
- salt and pepper to taste

Suggested wine: a dry, fruity white (Cerveteri Bianco)

This unusual sweet and sour dish comes from Gaeta in southern Lazio, where the influence of Middle Eastern cooking is strongest.

Basic recipes

For reasons of space I have moved a number of basic recipes to these pages. The Tomato Sauce is a classic and can be served with pasta, rice, potatoes, and in many other dishes. You can spice it up a little with a few slices of fresh chile pepper. The Clove-Flavored Meat Sauce (known as *Garofolato* in Italian) is an old Roman sauce; it is fairly time consuming and leaves you with a large piece of cooked meat as a by-product, but do try it at least once – it has a quite unique flavor. I have included a recipe for Meat Broth; although a bouillon cube dissolved in boiling water will often suffice, some broth and pasta dishes do call for a homemade broth. Finally, I have included instructions for making fresh pasta at home.

Tomato Sauce
For four, to serve with pasta and rice

2 cloves garlic, finely chopped
1 medium carrot, finely chopped
1 medium onion, finely chopped
1 stalk celery, finely chopped
2 tablespoons finely chopped parsley
4 tablespoons extra-virgin olive oil
2 cups/500 g fresh or canned tomatoes,
   skinned and coarsely chopped
salt and freshly ground black pepper
6 leaves fresh basil, torn

Sauté the garlic, carrot, onion, celery, and parsley in the oil for 4–5 minutes. ▪ Add the tomatoes. Season with salt and pepper. Simmer over low heat for at least 45 minutes, or until the sauce has reduced to the required density. ▪ Turn off the heat and stir in the basil. ▪ For a spicy sauce, add chile peppers to taste. ▪ In late summer, when tomatoes are plentiful, make a large quantity in a heavy-bottomed pan. Preserve in sterilized jars for use throughout the winter. When making large quantities of the sauce, simmer for at least 1½ hours.

Clove-Flavored Meat Sauce
For six, to serve with pasta

1¾ lb/800 g topside veal
3 oz/90 g lard, chopped
2 cloves garlic, finely chopped
salt and freshly ground black pepper
8–10 cloves
1 medium carrot, finely chopped
1 stalk celery, finely chopped
1 small onion, finely chopped
2 tablespoons finely chopped parsley
½ cup/125 ml dry white wine
½ cup/125 ml coarsely chopped canned tomatoes

Use a sharp knife to make 8–10 holes in the meat. Fill with half the lard and garlic and salt and pepper. Press a clove into each hole. ▪ Tie the meat using kitchen string and place in a pan. ▪ Sauté the remaining garlic in the remaining lard with the carrot, celery, onion, and parsley for 5 minutes. ▪ Add the vegetables and wine to the pan with the meat and cook over medium heat until the wine evaporates. ▪ Pour in the tomatoes and cover the meat with water. Partially cover the pan and cook until the sauce thickens (about 45 minutes). ▪ Use the sauce as directed in the recipes. The meat can be served separately as a main dish.

Meat Broth

This broth freezes very well, so make a large quantity, pour it into small containers (ice cube trays are ideal) so that it can be used as required. Makes about 1½ quarts/1.5 liters.

2½ lb/1¼ kg various cuts beef with bones
   (neck, shoulder, short ribs, brisket)
2 carrots
2 onions
1 large stalk celery
2 ripe tomatoes
2 cloves garlic
2 sprigs parsley
1 bay leaf
3 quarts/3 liters cold water

Put the meat, vegetables, and herbs in a large pot with the water. Cover and bring to the boil over medium heat. Season with salt and pepper. • Partially cover and simmer over low heat for 3 hours. • Turn off heat and leave to cool. • When the broth is cool, remove the vegetables and herbs, and skim off and discard the fat that will have formed on top.

Mixing plain pasta dough

For 4 generous servings you will need 2⅔ cups/400 g of all-purpose/plain flour and 4 medium eggs. Place the flour in a mound on a flat work surface and hollow out a well in the center. Break the eggs into the well one by one. Stir gently with a fork, gradually incorporating the flour. When the mixture is no longer runny, use your hands to finish mixing the flour with the eggs. Work the mixture until smooth, but quite firm. To test the mixture for the correct consistency, press a finger into the dough. If it comes out without any dough sticking to it, it is ready. If it is too moist, add more flour. If it is too dry, incorporate a little milk. Roll the mixture into a ball shape.

Kneading the dough

Clean the work surface of any excess dough and lightly sprinkle with flour. Push down and forwards on the ball of pasta dough with the heel of your palm. Fold the slightly extended piece of dough in half, give it a quarter-turn, and repeat the process. Continue for about 10 minutes or until the dough is very smooth. Place the ball of pasta dough on a plate and cover with an upturned bowl. Leave to rest for at least 15–20 minutes.

Rolling the dough out by hand

Place the ball of dough on a flat work surface and flatten with your hand. Place the rolling pin on the center of the ball and, applying light but firm pressure, roll the dough away from you. Give the ball a quarter-turn and repeat. When the dough has become a large round about ¼ in/5 mm thick, curl the far edge over the pin while holding the edge closest to you with your hand. Gently stretch the pasta. Unroll, give the dough a quarter-turn, and repeat. Continue rolling and stretching until transparent.

Rolling out using the pasta machine

Divide the dough into several pieces and flatten slightly with your hand. Set the machine with its rollers at their widest and run each piece through the machine. Reduce the rollers' width by one notch and repeat, reducing the rollers' width by one notch each time. Continue until all the pieces have gone through the machine at the thinnest roller setting. Cut to the widths indicated in the recipes.

Gnocchi del giovedì

Potato dumplings

Wash the potatoes thoroughly and cook in lightly salted boiling water with their skins on. ▪ Slip the skins off the cooked potatoes and mash them. Stir in the flour and salt. ▪ Beat the egg yolks with a fork until smooth. Add to the mixture and stir well until it is smooth. ▪ Take a handful of the mixture and roll it out on a lightly floured work surface using your hands. It should form a long sausage, about ½ in/1 cm in diameter. Use a sharp knife to cut the sausage into ¾-in/2-cm lengths. Repeat until all the mixture is used up. Place the little dumplings on a clean cloth to dry. Leave for at least 1 hour before cooking. ▪ Bring a large pot of salted water to a boil and add the dumplings in batches of about 30–40. When the dumplings have risen to the top, leave to bob around for about 2 minutes, then remove with a slotted spoon and place in a deep-sided serving bowl. Keep warm. Continue until all the dumplings are cooked. ▪ Pour the melted butter over the top and sprinkle with the parmesan. ▪ Serve at once.

Serves: 4–6
Preparation: 20 minutes + 1 hour's resting
Cooking: 25 minutes
Recipe grading: fairly easy

- 3 lb/1.5 kg potatoes
- ¾ cup/125 g all-purpose/plain flour
- salt
- 2 large egg yolks
- ½ cup/125 g butter, melted
- 1 cup/125 g freshly grated parmesan cheese, plus more parmesan to serve separately at the table

Suggested wine: a dry white (Frascati)

These little dumplings are served all over Italy. In Rome they are known as "Thursday's Dumplings" because they almost always appear on the menu on Thursday. Nobody quite knows why. For a more flavorsome sauce, add 6–8 leaves of fresh sage to the butter as you melt it.

Serves: 4
Preparation: 10 minutes
Cooking: 1 hour
Recipe grading: fairly easy

- 1 quart/1 liter milk
- 1⅔ cups/250 g semolina
- salt and freshly ground white pepper
- ½ cup/125 g butter
- 2 large egg yolks
- 1 cup/125 g freshly grated parmesan cheese, plus more parmesan to serve separately at the table
- 1 tablespoon grated gruyère cheese

Suggested wine: a light, dry rosato
(Frusinate Rosato)

Gnocchi alla romana

Baked semolina gnocchi

Bring the milk to a boil in a large, heavy-bottomed saucepan. ▪ Sprinkle the semolina in little by little, stirring all the time so that no lumps form. Keep stirring energetically for about 30 minutes, or until the mixture is dense. ▪ Remove from the heat and season with salt. Stir in half the butter, the egg yolks, half the parmesan, and the gruyère. ▪ Spread the mixture out to a thickness of about ½ in/1 cm on a flat, lightly floured work surface. Leave to cool. ▪ Use a glass to cut discs of the mixture. Butter an ovenproof dish and use the pieces leftover after cutting out the disks to form a first layer in the dish. Sprinkle with a little of the remaining parmesan. Lay the disks over the top, one overlapping the next. ▪ Melt the remaining butter and pour over the top. Sprinkle with the remaining parmesan and a grinding of pepper. ▪ Bake in a preheated oven at 350°F/180°C/gas 4 for about 30 minutes. The gnocchi should be a lovely golden color. ▪ Serve hot.

This delicious dish is known throughout Italy as "Gnocchi Roman-Style," even though it probably originated in Piedmont in the north. Children usually like gnocchi very much, so they are particularly suitable for a family meal.

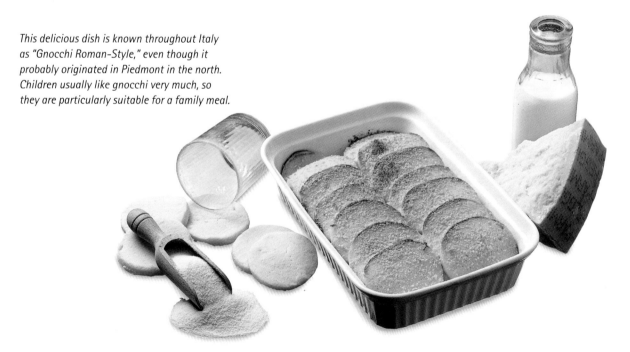

Penne alla ricotta

Penne with ricotta cheese

Warm the milk and place in a bowl with the ricotta, sugar, cinnamon, and a dash of salt and white pepper. Mix with a fork to form a smooth, creamy sauce. ▪ Cook the penne in a large pot of salted, boiling water until al dente. ▪ Drain well and place in a heated serving bowl. Toss with the sauce and serve.

Serves: 4
Preparation: 5 minutes
Cooking: about 10 minutes
Recipe grading: easy

- ¾ cup/180 ml whole milk
- 1 cup/250 g very fresh ricotta cheese
- 1 tablespoon sugar
- 1 teaspoon ground cinnamon
- salt and freshly ground white pepper
- 1 lb/500 g penne

Suggested wine: a dry, fruity white
(Colli Albani Secco)

This classic southern Italian recipe is very simple and relies on the quality and freshness of the ricotta. Buy it loose from a specialty store or a good Italian deli. It is also good with fresh pasta.

Zuppa di fave

Fava bean soup

Place the beans in a bowl and cover with cold water. Leave to soak for 12 hours. ▪ Drain the beans and cook in a pot of salted water for about 1 hour, or until they are tender. ▪ Heat the oil in a large heavy-bottomed pot (preferably earthenware) and sauté the pancetta, onion, celery, carrot, and marjoram (or parsley) until soft. ▪ Add the tomatoes and cook over a medium heat for 15 minutes. ▪ Add the prosciutto and cook for 2–3 minutes. ▪ Season with salt and pepper, then add the beans and 1 cup/250 ml of boiling water. Cook for 10 minutes, stirring frequently. ▪ Toast the bread and place a half slice in the bottom of 4 individual soup plates. Ladle the soup over the top and serve hot.

Serves: 4
Preparation: 10 minutes + 12 hours' soaking
Cooking: about 1¾ hours
Recipe grading: fairly easy

- 1¾ cups/350 g dried fava beans/ broad beans
- salt and freshly ground black pepper
- 4 tablespoons extra-virgin olive oil
- ½ cup/60 g diced pancetta
- 1 small onion, finely chopped
- 1 stalk celery, finely chopped
- 1 carrot, finely chopped
- 2 tablespoons finely chopped fresh marjoram (or parsley)
- generous ¾ cup/200 g peeled and chopped fresh or canned tomatoes
- 1 cup/125 g diced prosciutto/ Parma ham
- 2 large, thick slices day-old bread

Suggested wine: a young dry red
(Frascati Rosso)

Serves: 4
Preparation: 5 minutes + time to make the broth
Cooking: 30 minutes
Recipe grading: easy

- 1½ quarts/1.5 liters homemade meat broth (see recipe, page 49)
- 5 large eggs
- salt to taste
- dash of grated nutmeg
- 4 tablespoons freshly grated parmesan cheese, plus more parmesan to serve separately at the table

Suggested wine: a light, dry white (Castelli Romani)

Stracciatella alla romana

Meat broth with egg

Prepare the broth (or reheat it, if using frozen broth). ▪ Beat the eggs with a dash each of salt and nutmeg. Add the 4 tablespoons of parmesan and beat until smooth. ▪ When the broth is boiling, pour in the egg mixture. Beat with a fork for 3–4 minutes over a medium heat until the egg begins to cook and has formed lots of tiny lumps. ▪ Serve at once, with abundant parmesan on hand to pass around separately.

This simple, sustaining dish makes an excellent first course before serving boiled or roast meats.

Minestra di broccoli

Broccoli and tagliatelle soup

Wash the broccoli and trim the tough parts off the stalk. Dice the stalk and divide the tops into florets. ▪ Heat the oil in a large deep-sided pot and sauté the pork fat, garlic, and parsley for 4–5 minutes. ▪ Add the broccoli and cook for about 5 minutes. ▪ Add the tomato paste and water. Season with salt and pepper, then partially cover and cook over a medium-low heat for about 15 minutes, or until the broccoli is almost cooked. ▪ Add the tagliatelle and cook until it is al dente. ▪ Turn off the heat and leave for 3–4 minutes. ▪ Serve hot with the parmesan passed around separately.

Serves: 4
Preparation: 10 minutes
Cooking: 25 minutes
Recipe grading: easy

- 1 lb/500 g broccoli
- 2 tablespoons extra-virgin olive oil
- ¾ cup/90 g diced pork fat
- 2 cloves garlic, finely chopped
- 2 tablespoons finely chopped flat-leaf parsley
- 1 tablespoon concentrated tomato paste dissolved in ½ cup/125 ml warm water
- salt and freshly ground black pepper
- 8 oz/250 g tagliatelle, broken or cut into pieces
- 6 tablespoons freshly grated parmesan cheese

Suggested wine: a light, dry white (Est! Est!! Est!!!)

A healthy winter soup that the whole family will love.

Secondi piatti

With over two million sheep in the region, it is not surprising that lamb is an important dish in Lazio. Roasted with rosemary and potatoes, broiled (grilled), or stewed—lamb appears on the menu every day in the trattorias of Rome. Chicken, pork, veal, and beef are also popular, usually cooked or served with vegetables, such as bell peppers or artichokes. Seafood is served along the coast, from the ancient Etruscan town of Civitavecchia in the north to Gaeta in the south.

Pollo con peperoni

Chicken with bell peppers

Wash the chicken and pat it dry with a clean cloth. Cut into 8 pieces. ▪ Sauté the garlic in 2 tablespoons of the oil for 2–3 minutes, then add the tomatoes. Season with salt and pepper and cook over a moderate heat for 15 minutes, or until the sauce reduces. ▪ Clean the bell peppers, removing the seeds and core. Cut in quarters and place under the broiler (grill) until the skin blackens. ▪ Peel the blackened skin away with your fingers. Rinse the peppers and pat them dry. Cut into thin strips. ▪ Sauté the chicken in the remaining oil. Season with salt and pepper. Pour in the wine and cook over a moderate heat for 15 minutes. ▪ Add the tomato sauce and the bell peppers and cook together for 10 minutes more. ▪ Serve hot.

Serves: 4
Preparation: 10 minutes
Cooking: 45 minutes
Recipe grading: fairly easy

- 1 chicken, weighing about 2 lb/1 kg, cleaned
- 3 cloves garlic, finely chopped
- 8 tablespoons extra-virgin olive oil
- 1¾ cups/400 g peeled and chopped canned or fresh tomatoes
- salt and freshly ground black pepper
- 1 lb/500 g bell peppers/capsicums, mixed green, yellow, and red
- scant 1 cup/200 ml dry white wine

Suggested wine: a light, dry rosé (Sangiovese di Aprilia)

This dish is made throughout the summer and early fall, when bell peppers are at their tastiest and most plentiful. Try adding 7 oz/ 200 g of pitted whole black olives for even more flavor. The best black Gaeta olives are particularly recommended.

Saltimbocca alla romana

Braised veal and prosciutto slices

Serves: 4
Preparation: 10 minutes
Cooking: 5–6 minutes
Recipe grading: easy

- 8 thin slices of veal, weighing about 1 lb/500 g in total
- 8 leaves fresh sage
- 4 thin slices of prosciutto/Parma ham, weighing about 3½ oz/100 g in total, cut in half
- 4 tablespoons butter
- salt and freshly ground black pepper
- 4 tablespoons dry white wine

Suggested wine: a dry red
(Fiorano Rosso)

Beat the veal gently with a meat pounder, taking care not to pierce it. ▪ Place a leaf of sage at the center of each slice and cover with half a slice of prosciutto. Attach them to the veal using a toothpick, in the same way as you would use a safety pin. ▪ Melt the butter in a skillet (frying pan) large enough to hold the veal slices in a single layer. Add the veal, season with salt and pepper, and cook over a fairly high heat until done on one side. Drizzle with the wine and turn. Cook until the other side is done too. This should take only 5–6 minutes, otherwise the meat will become tough. ▪ Transfer the veal slices to a heated serving dish. Boil the remaining cooking juices for 1 minute, then pour over the veal. ▪ Serve hot.

Serve these tasty veal slices with potato purée and a green salad.

Serves: 4
Preparation: 5 minutes
Cooking: 25 minutes
Recipe grading: easy

- 2 cloves garlic, finely chopped
- ½ teaspoon crushed chile pepper (or 1 medium red fresh chile pepper, thinly sliced)
- 2 tablespoons extra-virgin olive oil
- 8 large Italian sausages
- 1½ lb/650 g flowering turnip tops (or broccoli, if preferred)
- salt and freshly ground black pepper

Suggested wine: a dry white (Orvieto)

Salsicce con broccoletti
Spicy sausages with flowering turnip tops

Sauté the garlic and chile pepper in the oil in a large skillet (frying pan) over a moderate heat until pale gold. ▪ Add the sausages and brown all over, pricking them here and there with the prongs of a fork to let some of the fat run out. ▪ Clean and wash the flowering turnip tops and add to the skillet. Season with salt and pepper. Cook for 20 minutes, or until the vegetables are tender, but not overcooked. Add a little water during cooking if the skillet dries out too much. ▪ Serve hot.

Flowering turnip tops, known as "broccoletti" in Italian, are a common winter vegetable in Lazio. You may substitute with the same amount of broccoli.

Costolette a scottadito

Broiled lamb chops

Serves: 4
Preparation: 5 minutes
Cooking: 15 minutes
Recipe grading: easy

- 2 lb/1 kg lamb chops
- 2 tablespoons extra-virgin olive oil (optional)
- salt and freshly ground black pepper

Suggested wine: a dry red
(Merlot d'Aprilia)

Place the chops on a large plate and drizzle with the oil, if using. Sprinkle with salt and a generous grinding of pepper. ▪ Arrange the chops in a grill pan and place over a high heat. Turn frequently until they are well-cooked all over. If you don't have a grill pan, arrange the chops on a wire rack and place under the broiler (grill). Turn frequently until they are done. ▪ Serve very hot.

These chops are even more delicious when cooked over a barbecue. Their Italian name "scottadito", means "finger burners" and refers to the fact that they are best eaten with your fingers.

Abbacchio al forno

Roast lamb and potatoes

Place the lamb in an ovenproof dish large enough to hold the lamb and the potatoes. ▪ Use the point of a sharp knife to make small incisions in the meat and push the pieces of garlic in. Close the meat around it, so that its flavor will permeate the meat during cooking. Run your hand backward up two of the rosemary sprigs and sprinkle the leaves over the lamb. Tuck the remaining sprigs in around the meat. Drizzle with the oil. Season with salt and pepper. ▪ Place in a preheated oven at 350°F/180°C/gas 4. ▪ Peel the potatoes and cut into large bite-sized chunks. Arrange them around the meat after it has been in the oven for about 20 minutes. ▪ The meat should take about 1 hour to cook, while the potatoes will need only about 40 minutes. Baste the meat with the cooking juices 2 or 3 times during roasting and turn the potatoes so that they are evenly browned. ▪ Serve hot.

Serves: 4
Preparation: 10 minutes
Cooking: 1 hour
Recipe grading: easy

- shoulder of baby lamb (with some loin attached), weighing about 2¼ lb/1.2 kg
- 2 cloves garlic, peeled and cut in half
- 4–6 sprigs fresh rosemary
- 4 tablespoons extra-virgin olive oil
- salt and freshly ground black pepper
- 2 lb/1 kg roasting potatoes

Suggested wine: a dry red
(Cerveteri Rosso)

Roast baby lamb with potatoes is a traditional dish at Easter in many parts of Italy.

Food in ancient Rome

In recent years the "Mediterranean diet" has become popular all over the world as people search for a healthy, low-cholesterol style of eating which is also appetizing. The origins of the Italian diet stretch back over 2,500 years to ancient Rome. Although many ingredients of modern Italian cuisine (the ubiquitous tomato is the most notable example) had not yet arrived from America, the basic diet of olive oil, wine, cheese, grains, fish, fruit, vegetables, and limited amounts of meat, was already in place. The ancient Romans had also discovered the importance of ambience for felicitous dining. Roman villas all had a dining room (wealthy people's villas had summer and winter dining rooms) with three long couches placed along the walls on which eight to ten people could recline comfortably as they ate, drank, and conversed. An inscription on the wall of a house in Pompeii has instructions for good behavior at evening parties: *Do not cast lustful glances or make eyes at another man's wife* (from which we learn that women were not banned from these parties as they were among the ancient Greeks in Athens). *Do not be coarse in your conversation. Restrain yourself from getting angry or using offensive language. If you cannot do so, then go home.*

Grapes, figs, and dates were basic foods. Besides being made into wine, grapes were eaten fresh or dried for consumption out of season.

Liquids such as olive oil and wine were transported and stored in large terracotta (baked earth) amphorae. The special Roman fish sauce known as "garum" was also stored in these containers. Garum was made from fish guts, heavily salted, and then allowed to ferment in large tanks. The resulting sauce (which must have been very tasty indeed!) was used to flavor stews and casseroles and many other dishes too.

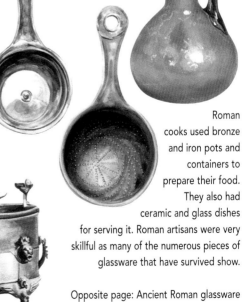

The streets and markets of ancient Roman towns were lined with shops selling bread, meat, fresh fruit and vegetables, as well as shoes, sandals, cloth, and other necessities. The ancient model above shows the proprietor of a fruit and vegetable store offering onions, garlic, and other fresh vegetables to his customers.

Italian painter G.P. Panini caught the "Grand Tour" spirit of the times in the early 18th century with his real and imaginary views of Roman ruins.

Right: An ancient Roman stove.

Roman cooks used bronze and iron pots and containers to prepare their food. They also had ceramic and glass dishes for serving it. Roman artisans were very skillful as many of the numerous pieces of glassware that have survived show.

Opposite page: Ancient Roman glassware

Serves: 4
Preparation: 10 minutes (+ 30 minutes
   soaking, if necessary)
Cooking: 5 minutes
Recipe grading: easy

- 3 lb/1.5 kg fresh mussels in shell
- 4 tablespoons extra-virgin olive oil
- 2 tablespoons finely chopped
  flat-leaf parsley
- 2 cloves garlic, finely chopped
- salt and freshly ground black pepper

Suggested wine: a light, dry white
(Marino Secco Superiore)

Zuppa di cozze
Mussel soup

Scrub the mussels well to remove their beards and rinse thoroughly under cold running water. If they appear to be holding a lot of sand, leave to soak in cold water for 30 minutes. ▪ Heat the oil in a large, deep-sided skillet (frying pan) and sauté the mussels until they are all open. Discard any that do not open. ▪ Sprinkle with the parsley and garlic. Season with salt and pepper and cook for 4–5 minutes more. ▪ Serve hot.

This dish is simplicity itself. To succeed, be sure to buy the very freshest of mussels. Serve with firm-textured bread, toasted briefly in a hot oven and drizzled with the highest quality extra-virgin olive oil.

Baccalà con peperoni

Salt cod with bell peppers

Skin the salt cod and remove the bones. Rinse under cold running water and pat dry with paper towels, then cut into pieces. ▪ Heat the frying oil in a large skillet (frying pan) until hot, but not smoking. ▪ Dip the salt cod in the flour until well coated. ▪ Fry in the oil until cooked. ▪ Drain on paper towels and set aside in a warm place. ▪ Sauté the onion in the extra-virgin olive oil in a deep-sided skillet until transparent. ▪ Add the tomatoes and cook over a moderate heat for 15 minutes, or until the sauce reduces. Season with salt and pepper. ▪ Clean the bell peppers, removing the seeds and core. Cut into quarters and place under the broiler (grill) until the skin blackens. Peel the blackened skin away with your fingers. Rinse the bell peppers and pat them dry. Cut into thin strips. ▪ Add the bell peppers and salt cod to the skillet with the tomato sauce. Cook together for 5 minutes, then serve.

Serves: 4
Preparation: 10 minutes
Cooking: 25 minutes
Recipe grading: easy

- 1¾ lb/800 g pre-soaked salt cod
- 1–2 cups/250–500 ml olive oil, for frying
- ⅔ cup/100 g all purpose/plain flour
- 1 large onion, finely chopped
- 4 tablespoons extra-virgin olive oil
- 1⅔ cups/400 g peeled and diced fresh or canned tomatoes
- 3 large bell peppers/capsicums, preferably 1 red, 1 yellow, 1 green
- salt and freshly ground black pepper

Suggested wine: a dry white
(Cerveteri Bianco)

Salt cod, a typically northern European dish, is popular all over Italy. It was adopted centuries ago after trading contacts were made with Holland and Scandinavia. In Rome it is usually served with a sweet and sour sauce, with bell peppers, or fried in a simple egg and flour batter.

Stufatino

Roman-style beef stew

Heat the pork fat in a large, heavy-bottomed pan and sauté the onion. When the onion turns pale gold, add the oil, garlic, and celery and sauté for 5 minutes. ▪ Add the beef and season with salt and pepper. Stir continually until the meat is lightly browned all over. ▪ Pour in the wine and cook until it evaporates. ▪ Add the tomatoes and cook for another 10 minutes, stirring frequently. ▪ Add enough cold water to cover the meat. Cover and cook over a low heat for at least 2 hours. The sauce should be thick and dark in color. ▪ Remove from the heat and stir in the marjoram or parsley just before serving. ▪ Serve hot.

Serves: 4
Preparation: 10 minutes
Cooking: about 2¼ hours
Recipe grading: easy

- ▪ ½ cup/60 g pork fat
- ▪ 1 large onion, finely chopped
- ▪ 2 tablespoons extra-virgin olive oil
- ▪ 2 cloves garlic, finely chopped
- ▪ 1 stalk celery, finely chopped
- ▪ 1 lb/500 g boneless beef chuck, cut into 1½-in/4-cm cubes
- ▪ salt and freshly ground black pepper
- ▪ scant ½ cup/100 ml dry white wine
- ▪ 2 large ripe tomatoes, peeled and diced
- ▪ 1 tablespoon finely chopped marjoram (or parsley)

Suggested wine: a dry red
(Cerveteri Rosso)

To freshen the dish a little, it is traditional to add 1 cup/100 g of coarsely chopped, lightly boiled celery stalks to the pot 5 minutes before serving. The stew is particularly good and hearty when served with boiled potatoes cooked briefly in tomato sauce (see recipe, page 48).

Serves: 4
Preparation: 15 minutes
Cooking: 1¼ hours
Recipe grading: easy

- 3 cloves garlic, finely chopped
- 1 tablespoon finely chopped
  rosemary leaves
- 4 leaves fresh sage
- 4 tablespoons extra-virgin olive oil
- 2 lb/1 kg tender young lamb shoulder,
  cut into 2-in/5-cm cubes with the bone
- salt and freshly ground black pepper
- 1 tablespoon all-purpose/plain flour
- scant ½ cup/100 ml white wine vinegar
- 4 tablespoons cold water
- 6 anchovy fillets

Suggested wine: a dry red
(Merlot d'Aprilia)

Abbacchio alla romana

Roman-style braised lamb

Sauté the garlic, rosemary, and sage in the oil in a large, deep-sided skillet (frying pan).
■ Add the lamb and season with salt and pepper. Stir in the flour, vinegar, and water.
Cover and cook over a low heat for 1 hour, adding extra water if the cooking liquid
dries out too much. ■ Put 2 tablespoons of the cooking liquid in a small bowl and
dissolve the anchovy fillets in it. Pour back into the stew and stir well. ■ Cook for
another 2–3 minutes, then remove from the heat and serve.

*This is one of the classics of Roman cooking.
It goes well with many vegetables, including
boiled potatoes, or Roman-style peas with
ham (see recipe, page 85), and Mixed
braised bell peppers (see recipe, page 92).*

Pollo con verdure

Braised chicken and vegetables

Sauté the onion and garlic in the oil in a large, deep-sided skillet (frying pan) until they turn pale gold. ▪ Add the chicken and brown all over. ▪ Pour in the wine and cook until it evaporates. ▪ Add the potatoes, carrots, celery, and parsley and season with salt and pepper. ▪ Pour in enough broth to moisten the dish, then cover and cook over a moderate heat for 25–30 minutes, stirring frequently. Add more broth as required during cooking. ▪ When the chicken is cooked and the vegetables tender, remove from the heat and serve.

Serves: 4
Preparation: 10 minutes
Cooking: 35 minutes
Recipe grading: easy

- 1 large onion, finely chopped
- 2 cloves garlic, finely chopped
- 4 tablespoons extra-virgin olive oil
- 1 chicken, about 3 lb/1.5 kg, cut into 8
- ½ cup/125 ml dry white wine
- 14 oz/400 g potatoes, peeled and coarsely chopped
- 4 medium carrots, coarsely chopped
- 2 stalks celery, coarsely chopped
- 2 tablespoons finely chopped parsley
- ⅔ cup/150 ml chicken broth
- salt and freshly ground black pepper

Suggested wine: a dry white (Orvieto)

Lamb – a Roman staple

The ancient Romans preferred kid (young goat's meat) over lamb; modern Romans have inverted this preference and lamb is now the most typical meat dish served. Known in the local dialect as "abbacchio" (from the verbs *abbacchiare* or *abbattere*, which mean "to butcher"), traditionally the most highly-prized lamb had to be less than a month old and still be fed on its mother's milk. Recently this very strict definition has been stretched a little and slightly older, weaned lambs are also served as *abbacchio*. Although fresh lamb is now available throughout the year, spring is the best season for it. *Abbacchio* is perhaps the most typical dish for Easter meals. Distinguishing real *abbacchio* from maturer meat is an art: it is not sufficient to check that the weight corresponds to the age of the animal – the meat itself has to be a very pale pink color. Darker meat raises doubts about the real age of the lamb. *Abbacchio* can be grilled, braised, roasted, or fried and is often served with potatoes. The lamb and artichoke recipe below combines two classic ingredients of Roman cooking.

Lamb with Artichokes
For four

4 large artichokes
juice of 1 lemon
2 oz/60 g prosciutto/Parma ham
2 cloves garlic
small bunch of parsley or marjoram
2 lb/1 kg lamb chops
1 small onion, finely chopped
½ cup/125 ml dry white wine
1 tablespoon tomato paste
salt and freshly ground black pepper

Clean the artichokes as explained on page 90. Cut in quarters and place in a bowl of cold water with the lemon juice. ▪ Finely chop the prosciutto, garlic, and parsley together and transfer to a large skillet (frying pan). Sauté for 3–4 minutes, then add the lamb chops and onion. Season with salt and pepper. ▪ When the onion is transparent, pour in the wine and cook until it has evaporated. ▪ Add the tomato paste and the drained artichokes. Cover, and cook over medium-low heat for about 15–20 minutes, or until the lamb and artichokes are tender. ▪ Serve hot.

The citizens of Rome have always been great lovers of lamb and all kinds of meat. Records from 1598 show that 73,000 lambs, 14,400 cows, 13,000 calves, 22,800 steers, 20,000 pigs, 818 piglets, and 600 oxen were officially butchered in the city during that year! The detailed records show the very strict control kept by city authorities.

The lamb is associated with Rome in more ways than one. The shepherd and the lamb are both traditional symbols of Christianity, and Rome has been the capital of Western Christendom for almost 2,000 years.

Lamb is usually butchered into three main parts called the "*coscia*" (leg), "*spalla*" (shoulder), and "*lombata*" (loin).

Nowadays there are over two million sheep in Lazio —Sardinia is the only Italian region with more of these animals.

Serves: 4
Preparation: 20 minutes
Cooking: 30 minutes
Recipe grading: fairly easy

- 1 calf's brain, about 1 lb/500 g
- 1 lb/500 g calf's liver, cut in slices
  ½ in/1 cm thick
- 4–6 globe artichokes
- juice of 1 lemon
- 4–8 slices firm-textured bread
- about 4 tablespoons milk
- 1–2 cups/250–500 ml olive oil, for frying
- 1 cup/150 g all-purpose/plain flour
- 3 large eggs, lightly beaten
- salt

Suggested wine: a dry red
(Sangiovese d'Aprilia)

Fritto misto

Mixed fried meat, vegetables, and bread

Wash the calf's brains thoroughly under cold running water, then soak in a bowl of cold water for 10 minutes. ▪ Place in a pot of cold water and boil for 20 minutes. Remove all the brown parts and cut the brain into 6 pieces. ▪ Cut the calf's liver into pieces about 1¼ x 1½ in/3 x 4 cm. ▪ Clean the artichokes by trimming the tops and stalk (leave about ¼ in/1 cm of stalk attached). Remove all the tough outer leaves so that only the pale, inner part remains. Cut each artichoke into quarters. As you clean the artichokes, place them in a large bowl of cold water with the lemon juice (this will stop them from discoloring). Drain well and pat dry. ▪ Place the bread on a plate and drizzle with the milk. The slices should be damp, but not soggy. ▪ Heat the oil in a deep-sided skillet (frying pan) until hot, but not smoking. ▪ Dip the meats, artichokes, and bread in the flour, then in the egg. Fry in the oil, turning frequently, until golden brown all over. Drain on paper towels. Don't try to fry too much at once. The pieces of meat and artichokes should not touch one another. ▪ Season with salt and serve immediately.

These are the three most traditional ingredients in a Roman Fritto Misto, *but you can use many others as well. Most meats fry well, as do vegetables. Onions, cauliflower, and zucchini (courgettes) are particularly suitable. The wonderful crisp fried bread is known as "pandorato" – "golden bread" – in Rome.*

Trippa alla trasteverina

Trastevere-style baked tripe

Heat the oil in a skillet (frying pan) and add the carrot, onion, celery, and garlic. Sauté for 5 minutes. ▪ Add the tomatoes. Sauté over a medium heat for 5–10 minutes more. ▪ Cut the tripe into large diamond shapes. ▪ Pour a little of the sauce into the bottom of a deep-sided ovenproof dish and cover with a layer of tripe. Sprinkle with some of the cheese and mint. Repeat this process until all the ingredients are used up. Make sure you finish with a layer of cheese. ▪ Bake in a preheated oven at 350°F/180°C/gas 4 for 30 minutes. ▪ Serve hot with a little extra cheese and mint sprinkled over the top, if liked.

Serves: 4
Preparation: 10 minutes
Cooking: 40 minutes
Recipe grading: easy

- 4 tablespoons extra-virgin olive oil
- 1 carrot, finely chopped
- 1 onion, finely chopped
- 1 stalk celery, finely chopped
- 2 cloves garlic, finely chopped
- 4 tablespoons peeled and diced fresh or canned tomatoes
- 2 lb/1 kg ready-to-cook, calf's honeycomb tripe
- 1¼ cups/150 g freshly grated pecorino romano cheese
- 8–10 leaves fresh mint, torn

Suggested wine: a light, dry red
(Genazzano Rosso)

The traditional recipe calls for the rather special Clove-Flavored Meat Sauce (see recipe, page 49). Because you may not always have this on hand, we have given a modern, easy-to-make recipe for the sauce.

Serves: 2–4
Preparation: 5 minutes
Cooking: 10 minutes
Recipe grading: easy

- 6 large eggs
- 2 tablespoons diced pancetta
- 2 tablespoons diced mozzarella cheese
- 1 tablespoon finely chopped shallots
- salt and freshly ground black pepper
- 4 tablespoons butter

Suggested wine: a dry rosé
(Viganello Rosato)

Frittata alla ciociara
Frosinone omelet

Mix the eggs, pancetta, mozzarella, shallots, salt, and pepper in a mixing bowl. ▪ Heat two-thirds of the butter over a moderate heat in a medium-sized skillet (frying pan) until it turns light gold. ▪ Pour in the egg mixture and stir for a few seconds. Cook until golden brown underneath. ▪ Turn the half-cooked omelet out onto a large plate. ▪ Add the remaining butter to the skillet. When it turns gold, return the omelet to the skillet with the other side underneath and cook until golden brown. ▪ When the egg is cooked (dry, but not overcooked), slip the omelet onto a heated dish and serve at once.

*Easy to prepare and tasty, Frosinone omelet makes an
excellent light lunch. Serve it with a green salad.*

Fish

The Tyrrhenian Sea that washes the shores of Lazio is teeming with seafood of every kind. The city of Rome gets its fish fresh every morning from the tiny port of Fiumicino on the coast. By lunchtime many of the bustling restaurants of the capital

aristocracy or in convents and other Christian places, where the consumption of meat was limited for religious reasons. The advent of refrigeration and efficient transportation after World War II made seafood available for people who lived inland.

have a good selection of seafood dishes on their menus. This is a relatively new development, since fish were not so popular in Rome until around 50 years ago. Up until then they were mostly served in the homes of the

The coastal villages and towns, from Civitavecchia in the north to Gaeta in the south, have always relied on the sea and fish is an important part of the coastal diet and culinary traditions.

Local fishermen ply the coastal waters with their nets in the early hours of the morning. The water is fairly clean and the quality of the catch is generally excellent. This is not so in the Tiber River that runs through Rome, which is very polluted. Although there are still many fish in the river and fishing competitions are common along its banks, the fish themselves are not fit for human consumption.

Molluscs and crustaceans, including shrimp, calamari, octopus, clams, and mussels, are known collectively as *"frutti di mare"* (fruits of the sea) in Italian. They are often cooked quickly in a pan or grill and served with a simple dressing made with extra-virgin olive oil, garlic, parsley, and salt and pepper. This method is only successful if using the freshest seafood. Frozen *frutti di mare* are not recommended in this case.

Untangling the nets after a successful morning's fishing.

Beautiful Lake Bolsena has trout, pike, tench, whitefish, mullet, and eels to offer the inhabitants of the surrounding villages. These fish are prepared in a wide variety of ways; fettuccine pasta with peas cooked in tench broth is one of the most typical (and delicious!) local dishes.

Verdure

Globe artichokes are the emblematic vegetable in Roman cooking. When you step into a trattoria, you will see them raw, piled high on platters, or cooked, stem up in earthenware dishes. Beyond the sprawling suburbs of the capital, Lazio is an agricultural region and a large variety of vegetables are produced throughout the year. Romaine lettuce is widely cultivated, as are bell peppers, green beans, peas, and baby onions. Gathered in the afternoon and sold early next morning, the quality is excellent because they are so fresh.

Piselli alla romana

Roman-style peas with ham

Sauté the onion in the lard (or butter) over a medium heat until it turns pale gold. ▪ Add the peas and broth. Season with salt and pepper and cook for 10 minutes, or until the peas are tender. ▪ Add the prosciutto 2 minutes before the peas are cooked. ▪ Serve hot.

Serves: 4
Preparation: 5 minutes
Cooking: about 10 minutes
Recipe grading: easy

- 1 small onion, finely chopped
- 4 tablespoons lard (or butter)
- 1½ lb/750 g fresh shelled (or frozen) sweet young peas
- scant ½ cup/100 ml meat broth (homemade or bouillon cube)
- salt and freshly ground black pepper
- 3 oz/90 g prosciutto/Parma ham, cut in one thick slice, then diced

Suggested wine: a dry white
(Frascati Novello)

This is a classic Roman side dish. The peas from the region of Lazio are small and sweet. You may need to add a dash of sugar if you are using larger, tougher peas.

Serves: 4
Preparation: 10 minutes
Cooking: 20 minutes
Recipe grading: easy

- 8 large globe artichokes
- juice of 1 lemon
- 1 cup/250 ml extra-virgin olive oil
- salt

Suggested wine: a dry red
(Colli Albani)

Carciofi alla giudia

Jewish-style artichokes

Clean the artichokes by trimming the tops and stalk (leave about 1½ in/4 cm of stalk attached). Remove all the tough outer leaves so that only the pale, inner part remains. As you clean the artichokes, place them in a large bowl of cold water with the lemon juice (this will stop them from discoloring). ▪ Drain and bang each artichoke down on the bench so that the leaves open out a little. ▪ Heat the oil in a large skillet (frying pan) and add the artichokes. Cook over a medium heat for 15–20 minutes. ▪ When the artichokes are tender, turn up the heat and brown them for 2–3 minutes. They should turn a lovely golden brown at this stage. ▪ Drain on paper towels, season with salt, and serve at once.

Artichokes are a staple vegetable in Rome during the winter months and are prepared in myriad ways. This is one of the heartiest dishes.

Eating in Rome

Romans love to eat out and the city is packed with cafés, *enoteche* (wine bars), pizzerias, pubs, trattorias, and restaurants. With only a little effort at getting off the beaten track, visitors can sample the delights of Roman cooking alongside the locals. With the exception of the Chinese restaurants that have mushroomed over the last decade, most eateries offer Roman food, or specialties from other regions of Italy. The quality is generally very high and the prices more than reasonable. The *enoteche* or wine bars

that now dot the streets of Rome are a relatively new addition to the culinary cityscape and are really worth a try. Here you can get smallish servings of hot or cold dishes served with an excellent glass of wine. These places have sprung up in the last 20 to 30 years as daily lunchtimes have dwindled from three hour siestas to 30 minute breaks. The food served is generally excellent and the choice and quality of the wines usually impeccable. The more informal surroundings attract a younger, wealthier, and less traditional clientele.

"When in Rome, do as the Romans do" — particularly at breakfast time. This means you can start the day with a variety of pastries and a delicious cappuccino.

There is nothing new about dining out in Rome; the locals have been at it for over 2,000 years. The painting (top left) shows the doorway of a trattoria serving Castelli wine during the 18th century. The larger one (left), shows a scene in a typical restaurant in the 19th century.

Romans know that fresh, high quality ingredients are the key to good cooking and excellent food. Even crowded, expensive, central Rome has its street markets so that the locals can buy what they need. Campo de' Fiori is certainly the largest and probably the most beautiful of them all. Every morning except Sunday, the old piazza bustles with stalls selling fruit, vegetables, fish, cheeses, and other produce. Nearby delicatessens and bakeries offer excellent bread and other specialties.

No visit to Rome would be complete without sampling a *porchetta* (roast pork) sandwich or roll. Whole pigs are stuffed with salt and spices and then cooked. Thick slices of pork between two slabs of bread make a hearty lunch or snack.

Serves: 4
Preparation: 10 minutes
Cooking: 35 minutes
Recipe grading: easy

- 8 medium artichokes
- juice of 1 lemon
- 1 onion, finely chopped
- 2 tablespoons extra-virgin olive oil
- 4 tablespoons diced prosciutto/ Parma ham (optional)
- salt and freshly ground black pepper
- 3 cups/375 g fresh shelled (or frozen) peas

Suggested wine: a dry red (Castelli Romani)

Carciofi con piselli

Artichokes and peas

Clean the artichokes by trimming the tops and stalk. Remove all the tough outer leaves so that only the pale, inner part remains. Cut each artichoke in half and place in a large bowl of cold water with the lemon juice (this will stop them from discoloring). ▪ Sauté the onion in the oil in a large skillet (frying pan) until pale gold. Add the prosciutto, if using. ▪ Drain the artichokes and add them to the skillet. Cook for 10 minutes, or until they are tender. ▪ Season with salt and pepper and add the peas. Cook over medium heat for about 15–20 minutes, or until the peas and artichokes are both tender. Add a little cold water as necessary to keep the vegetables moist. ▪ Serve hot or at room temperature.

The peas and artichokes together make a rich and nourishing dish. This recipe is ideal for vegetarians (without the prosciutto) and can be served, with bread and salad, as a light lunch.

Melanzane ripiene

Stuffed eggplants

Serves: 4
Preparation: 20 minutes
Cooking: 30 minutes
Recipe grading: easy

Rinse the eggplants thoroughly under cold running water and slice them in half. Use a sharp knife to hollow out the flesh, taking care not to pierce the skins. ▪ Dice the eggplant flesh and combine with the mozzarella and garlic (if using). Drizzle with 2 tablespoons of the oil and season with salt and pepper. Mix well. ▪ Arrange the hollowed-out eggplant halves in a shallow, ovenproof dish. Fill with the mozzarella mixture. Spoon the chopped tomato over the top. ▪ Bake in a preheated oven at 350°F/180°C/gas 4 for about 30 minutes. ▪ Serve hot or at room temperature.

- 4 small eggplants/aubergines
- 8 oz/250 g mozzarella cheese, cut into ½ in/1 cm dice
- 1 clove garlic, finely chopped (optional)
- 3 tablespoons extra-virgin olive oil
- salt and freshly ground black pepper
- 3 large ripe tomatoes, peeled and diced

Suggested wine: a dry white
(Cerveteri Bianco)

These eggplants are so simple to prepare yet they are always a success. Serve them as a side dish or an appetizer. Add a few torn basil leaves to the tomato mixture for extra flavor.

Serves: 4–6
Preparation: 10 minutes
Cooking: 25 minutes
Recipe grading: easy

- 4–6 bell peppers/capsicums
  (mixed red, green, and yellow),
  cut into ½-in/1-cm strips
- 2 large onions, thinly sliced
- 2 cups/500 g peeled and chopped
  fresh or canned tomatoes
- 4 tablespoons extra-virgin olive oil
- 3 cloves garlic, finely chopped
- salt and freshly ground black pepper
- 6 leaves fresh basil, torn

Suggested wine: a light, dry white
(Frascati)

Peperonata

Mixed braised bell peppers

Place the vegetables in a large heavy-bottomed saucepan or earthenware pot. Add the oil and garlic and season with salt and pepper. Cover and cook over a medium heat for about 15 minutes. ▪ Turn the heat up to high and partially uncover to let some of the liquid evaporate. Cook until the bell peppers are tender. ▪ Garnish with basil leaves and serve hot or at room temperature.

This classic dish is delicious when cooked in an earthenware pot. For a stronger, more distinctive flavor, add 1 medium eggplant (aubergine), diced but not peeled, 1½ cups/150 g of pitted black olives, and 1 teaspoon of oregano.

Serves: 4
Preparation: 20 minutes
Cooking: 30 minutes
Recipe grading: easy

- 1½ lb/650 g fresh or 14 oz/400 g frozen spinach
- generous ¾ cup/200 g ricotta cheese
- 2 tablespoons all-purpose/plain flour plus extra for flouring
- 2 large eggs
- salt and freshly ground black pepper
- 1 cup/250 ml olive oil, for frying

Suggested wine: a dry white
(Colli Albani)

Polpette di spinaci e ricotta

Spinach and ricotta croquettes

If using fresh spinach, trim the stalks and rinse well under cold running water. ▪ Place the spinach in a small pan of salted water and cook over a medium high heat for 7–10 minutes, or until tender. ▪ Drain well and squeeze out all the excess moisture. Transfer to a chopping board and chop finely. ▪ Combine the spinach in a bowl with the ricotta, flour, eggs, salt, and pepper and mix well. ▪ Heat the oil in a skillet (frying pan) until very hot, but not smoking. ▪ Shape spoonfuls of the spinach mixture into walnut-sized balls and roll them in the extra flour. ▪ Fry the croquettes in the oil, turning them frequently, until they are crisp and well-cooked. ▪ Drain on paper towels. Season with a little salt and serve at once.

Zucchine marinate
Marinated zucchini

Wash the zucchini under cold running water and trim the ends off. Dry well with paper towels. Cut the zucchini into wheels. ▪ Heat the oil in a large skillet (frying pan) and fry the zucchini wheels in 2 or 3 batches for 7–8 minutes. ▪ Place the cooked zucchini in a deep-sided dish. ▪ Heat the vinegar with the salt and chile pepper until it begins to boil. Pour over the zucchini. ▪ Season with a generous grinding of black pepper and cover. Set aside for 24 hours before use. ▪ Serve at room temperature.

Serves: 6
Preparation: 5 minutes
Cooking: 25 minutes
Recipe grading: easy

- 8 large zucchini/courgettes
- 4 tablespoons extra-virgin olive oil
- 1 cup/250 ml white wine vinegar
- salt and freshly ground black pepper
- 1 red chile pepper

Suggested wine: a light, dry white
(Est! Est!! Est!!!)

Serves: 4
Preparation: 15 minutes + 20 minutes'
resting
Cooking: about 20 minutes
Recipe grading: easy

- 3 large potatoes
- salt and freshly ground black pepper
- ½ medium Savoy cabbage
- 2 tablespoons extra-virgin olive oil
- 1 small onion, finely chopped
- ½ cup/60 g diced pancetta
- 1 clove garlic, finely chopped
- ½ teaspoon crushed chile pepper

Suggested wine: a light, dry white (Frascati)

Patate e cavoli

Potato and cabbage mix

Cook the potatoes in a large pot of salted, boiling water. Peel and mash them. ▪ Boil the cabbage in another pot of salted water for 10 minutes. Drain well and chop coarsely. ▪ Heat the oil in a large skillet (frying pan) and sauté the onion until pale gold. Add the pancetta, garlic, and chile pepper. Season with salt and pepper, then add the potatoes and cabbage. ▪ Mix well and then set aside for about 20 minutes to absorb the flavors. ▪ Serve warm or at room temperature.

Serves: 6
Preparation: 20 minutes
Cooking: 30 minutes
Recipe grading: easy

- 14 oz/400 g porcini mushrooms
- 1 cup/250 ml olive oil, for frying
- 1 cup/150 g all-purpose/plain flour
- salt

Suggested wine: a dry white
(Colli Albani)

Funghi dorati

Fried porcini mushrooms

Wash the mushrooms under cold running water and pat dry with paper towels. Trim off the roots and discard. Slice the stalks and heads. ▪ Heat the oil in a large skillet (frying pan) until very hot, but not smoking. ▪ Dip the mushrooms in the flour and then fry in the oil, turning frequently, until golden brown. ▪ Drain on paper towels and sprinkle with a little salt (if liked). ▪ Serve at once.

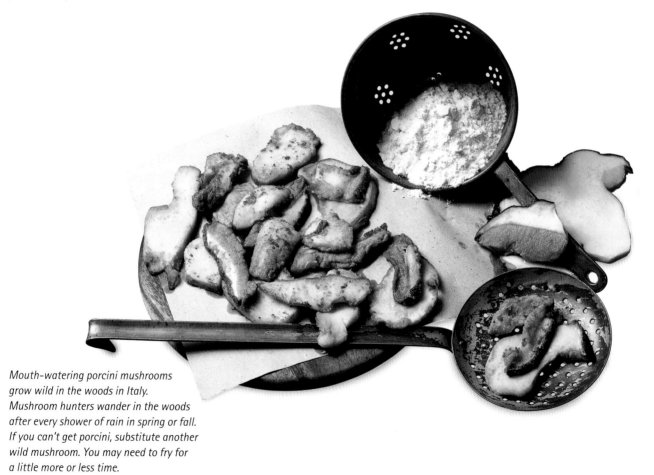

Mouth-watering porcini mushrooms grow wild in the woods in Italy. Mushroom hunters wander in the woods after every shower of rain in spring or fall. If you can't get porcini, substitute another wild mushroom. You may need to fry for a little more or less time.

Cipolline in agrodolce

Sweet and sour baby onions

Serves: 4–6
Preparation: 10 minutes
Cooking: 35 minutes
Recipe grading: easy

Clean the onions and place them in a bowl of cold water. ▪ Sauté the prosciutto in the lard (or butter or oil) in a medium saucepan. ▪ Drain the onions and add to the pan. Season with salt and pepper and add the sugar. Pour in the vinegar and water. ▪ Cook over a medium-low heat until the onions are tender and the cooking juices have almost all been absorbed. ▪ Serve hot or at room temperature.

- 1 lb/500 g white baby onions
- ½ cup/60 g diced prosciutto/Parma ham
- 1 tablespoon lard (or butter or extra-virgin olive oil)
- salt and freshly ground black pepper
- 1 tablespoon sugar
- 3 tablespoons white wine vinegar
- scant ½ cup/100 ml cold water

Suggested wine: a light, dry white (Colli Albani)

Dolci

Cakes, cookies, and desserts are less of a feature in Roman cooking than in many other regions of Italy. Cooks in the Eternal City have gladly adopted dishes from other regions and countries and a typical trattoria will offer a variety of dishes from other parts of Italy and abroad. However, there are a limited number of traditional dishes, usually linked to feast days or specific towns in Lazio, which are well worth trying. As in many other regions, fritters are always popular, and are also linked to seasons or feast days.

Fette di mele fritte

Sliced apple fritters

Separate the eggs and beat the yolks in a bowl until smooth. ▪ Add the flour, wine, extra-virgin olive oil, and salt and mix to obtain a smooth, fairly liquid batter. Cover the bowl and set aside to rest for 1 hour. ▪ Peel and core the apples, leaving them whole. Slice crosswise and drizzle with the lemon juice to stop them turning black. ▪ Heat enough oil to cover the bottom of a large skillet (frying pan) until very hot, but not smoking. ▪ Beat the egg whites until they form stiff peaks. Stir into the batter. ▪ Dip the apple slices into the batter and fry in batches until light golden brown on both sides. Don't put too many slices in the pan at once or they will stick together. Repeat until all the apples are used up. ▪ Place the fried slices on paper towels to drain. Keep them on a warm plate as you finish the rest. ▪ Sprinkle with confectioners' sugar and serve immediately.

Serves: 4–6
Preparation: 10 minutes + 1 hour's resting
Cooking: 15 minutes
Recipe grading: fairly easy

- 2 large eggs
- ¾ cup/125 g all-purpose/plain flour
- ½ cup/125 ml dry white wine
- 2 tablespoons extra-virgin olive oil
- dash of salt
- 6 cooking apples
- juice of 1 lemon
- olive oil, for frying
- confectioners'/icing sugar

Suggested wine: a sweet white
(Cesanese del Piglio Dolce)

Simple and elegant, this dessert goes very well with vanilla ice cream or whipped cream. Be sure to keep the apples hot until you serve them. Ideally, they should be served as soon after cooking as possible.

Maritozzi

Candied fruit and pine nut buns

Crumble the yeast into a small bowl with 5 tablespoons of the water, stirring until the yeast dissolves. ▪ Leave to stand for 10 minutes in a warm (not hot) place until the surface is frothy. ▪ Place about one-third of the flour in a mixing bowl and stir in the yeast mixture. Transfer the dough to a floured work surface and knead to obtain a smooth dough. Cover with a clean cloth and set aside to rise for about 3 hours. ▪ Transfer the risen dough to a lightly floured work surface and knead in the remaining flour, the oil, sugar, golden raisins, pine nuts, candied fruit, and salt. Add the remaining water as required to obtain a firm, moist dough. Knead thoroughly. Break the dough into bread roll-size buns and place, well spaced, on an oiled baking sheet. Cover with a clean cloth and set aside to rise for another 4 hours. ▪ Bake in a preheated oven at 350°F/180°C/gas 4 for about 15 minutes, or until they are well-cooked inside and golden brown on the outside.

Serves: 6
Preparation: 30 minutes + 7 hours' rising
Cooking: about 15 minutes
Recipe grading: fairly easy

- 1 oz/30 g fresh compressed/baker's yeast or 3 packets active dried yeast
- scant 1 cup/200 ml warm water
- 2 cups/300 g all-purpose/plain flour
- 2 tablespoons extra-virgin olive oil
- ¼ cup/50 g superfine/caster sugar
- ⅓ cup/100 g golden raisins/sultanas, soaked in warm water for 15 minutes, well-drained
- 3 tablespoons pine nuts
- 1½ tablespoons chopped candied orange and lemon peel
- dash of salt

Suggested wine: a sweet or medium dessert wine (Marino Amabile or Dolce)

Maritozzi *were traditionally offered to family and guests during Lent with a glass of sweet or dry white wine.*

Serves: 4
Preparation: 5 minutes + 1 hour's resting
Recipe grading: easy

- 1¼ lb/625 g fresh strawberries
- 6 tablespoons superfine/caster sugar
- ½ cup/125 ml dry white wine

Suggested wine: a light, dry white (Frascati)

Fragole al vino bianco

Strawberries in white wine

Clean the strawberries and rinse under cold running water. Drain well, then pat dry with a clean dishcloth. ▪ Transfer the strawberries to a serving dish. Sprinkle with the sugar and drizzle with the wine. ▪ Place in the refrigerator to rest for at least 1 hour before serving.

Healthy and delicious on their own, these strawberries are excellent when served with vanilla ice cream. They make a refreshing dessert at the end of dinner on warm, early summer nights when the strawberry season is at its peak. Try replacing the wine with the same amount of white wine vinegar for even more taste.

Crema di ricotta

Ricotta cream

Put the ricotta in a mixing bowl and stir in the confectioners' sugar and cinnamon. Mix well to obtain a smooth, light cream. ▪ Place in the refrigerator to rest for at least 1 hour before serving.

Serves: 4
Preparation: 5 minutes + 1 hour's resting
Recipe grading: easy

- 1¼ lb/625 g fresh ricotta cheese
- 6 tablespoons confectioners'/icing sugar
- 1 teaspoon freshly ground cinnamon

Suggested wine: a dry, sparkling white
(Colli Albani Spumante Secco)

This recipe calls for the very freshest of ricotta cheese. Don't even attempt to make it with the ricotta cheeses prepacked in plastic containers. You can replace the cinnamon with ½ teaspoon of vanilla extract, or 2 tablespoons of unsweetened cocoa powder.

Serves: 8–10
Preparation: 30 minutes (+ overnight rising +
3 hours' rising)
Cooking: 40 minutes
Recipe grading: complicated

- 1½ oz/45 g fresh compressed/baker's
  yeast or 4½ packets active dried yeast
- about 5 tablespoons water
- 3 cups/450 g all-purpose/plain flour
- 7 large eggs
- ¾ cup/150 g superfine/caster sugar
- 4 tablespoons fresh ricotta cheese
- scant ½ cup/100 ml rum
- scant ½ cup/100 ml milk
- 1 teaspoon ground cinnamon
- ½ teaspoon crushed aniseeds
- grated zest of 1 lemon
- scant ½ cup/100 g lard (or butter),
  softened
- 5 tablespoons confectioners'/icing sugar

Suggested wine: a sweet dessert wine
(Aleatico di Gradoli)

Pizza dolce civitavecchiese
Civitavecchia sweet pizza

Crumble the yeast into a small bowl with the water, stirring until the yeast dissolves. ▪ Leave to stand for 10 minutes in a warm (not hot) place until the surface is frothy. ▪ Put about a quarter of the flour in a mixing bowl and stir in the yeast mixture. Transfer to a lightly floured work surface and knead to obtain a smooth dough. Form the dough into a ball, then cover with a clean cloth and set aside to rise overnight. ▪ Next morning, separate the eggs and beat 6 yolks with the sugar in a large mixing bowl until smooth and creamy. ▪ Whisk the 7 egg whites until they form stiff peaks. ▪ Stir the ricotta, rum, milk, egg whites, cinnamon, aniseed, and lemon zest into the egg yolk and sugar mixture. ▪ Mix well, then add the risen dough, the remaining flour, and the lard (or butter). Turn the mixture out onto a floured work surface and knead for about 10 minutes. Form the dough into a ball, then cover with a clean cloth and set aside in a warm place to rise for 2 hours. ▪ Knead again for a few minutes, and form into a ball. Set aside as before to rise for 1 hour. ▪ Place the dough in a large buttered springform pan (tin). Beat the remaining egg yolk and pour it over the top. Sprinkle with the confectioners' sugar. ▪ Bake in a preheated oven at 325°F/170°C/gas 3 for 40 minutes or until well browned on top. ▪ Remove from the springform pan and leave to cool.

Making this special cake is a marathon job,
but well worth the effort!

Sformato al cioccolato

Chocolate mold

Serves: 6
Preparation: 30 minutes
Cooking: 25 minutes
Recipe grading: fairly easy

- ½ cup/75 g all-purpose/plain flour
- 1 cup/250 ml milk
- ½ cup/100 g superfine/caster sugar
- 4 tablespoons butter
- 4 large eggs, separated
- 5 tablespoons unsweetened cocoa powder

Suggested wine: a dry sparkling white (Frascati Spumante)

Mix the flour in a little of the milk until smooth. ▪ Bring the remaining milk to a boil in a heavy-bottomed saucepan with the sugar and butter. Stir in the flour mixture and mix well. Remove from the heat and set aside to cool. ▪ Beat the egg yolks until creamy. ▪ Whisk the egg whites until they form stiff peaks. ▪ Add the cocoa powder to the cooled milk mixture and mix well. ▪ Stir in the egg yolks, then fold the egg whites in carefully. ▪ Butter and flour a ring mold and pour the mixture into it. ▪ Bake in a preheated oven at 375°F/190°C/gas 5 for 25 minutes. ▪ Remove from the oven and set aside to cool. Turn out of the ring mold and serve.

This delicious mold will be a hit with all chocolate lovers. If liked, it can be kept in the refrigerator for a few hours before serving.

La dolce vita

Italian film director Federico Fellini immortalized the life and times of the international set of "beautiful" people in Rome in the late 1950s in his satirical film *La Dolce Vita* (1960). During the 1950s and 60s Rome became the Hollywood of Europe, particularly as American film makers took advantage of lower costs and taxes by making their films in Italy. This is the era of the "Spaghetti Western". The actors, actresses, directors, and film crews that flocked to the city added another dimension to the capital's social and nightlife which was already populated by a heterogenous group of Italian and European artists and intellectuals. Much of the action was centered on Via Veneto, which at that time was a smart area with upmarket hotels, restaurants, and cafés. (It has since lost its position as the meeting place of the idle rich and the famous). The Piazza di Spagna area, also mentioned in the film, is still a lively part of town with some excellent shopping (the via Condotti is perhaps the most famous area for fashion and design) as well as cafés and restaurants. Both the Via Veneto and Piazza di Spagna quarters are still popular today, although some other new areas have opened up in the meantime. The narrow streets and charming piazzas of Trastevere, and the areas around Piazza Navona, and the Pantheon are always good bets for food and nightlife.

During the 18th century, when Rome was one of the focal points of the Grand Tour taken by well-to-do Europeans, the area around Piazza di Spagna (the Spanish Steps) was the "in" place to be seen. Then, as now, both tourists and locals spent a lot of time in the cafés, chatting, and people-watching.

The film poster from *La Dolce Vita*, which starred blonde bombshell Anita Ekberg and handsome Marcello Mastroiani.

In a city of fountains the Trevi Fountain (above) is perhaps the most famous of them all. Traditionally the spot to toss a coin over one's back while making the wish to return again to Rome, it was made even more famous by Fellini's film. It was here that Anita Ekberg took her cooling midnight dip with Mastroiani in attendance.

The Café de Paris (above) opened its doors in Via Veneto in 1956. It was one of the best cafés during the area's heyday. The whole area is (at least in Roman terms) quite recent; most of it was laid out after Rome became capital of Italy in 1870. A restaurant called George's at number 7 in Via Marche (parallel to Via Veneto) is another good place to capture some of the flavor of the *dolce vita* times.

Big names in the Italian fashion world line the streets of central Rome.

Serves: 6
Preparation: 15 minutes + 1 hour's resting
Cooking: 25 minutes
Recipe grading: easy

- 2 cups/300 g all-purpose/plain flour
- 1 cup/200 g superfine/caster sugar
- 2–3 drops vanilla extract/essence
- 1 teaspoon ground cinnamon
- finely grated zest of 1 lemon
- 1 teaspoon baking powder
- 3 tablespoons extra-virgin olive oil
- 2 large eggs

Suggested wine: a sweet white
(Orvieto Dolce)

Ciambelline dolci

Sweet rings

Place the flour, sugar, vanilla, cinnamon, lemon zest, and baking powder in a mixing bowl. Stir in the oil and eggs and mix for about 5–8 minutes with a wooden spoon. Cover with a clean cloth and leave to rest for 1 hour. ▪ Lightly flour a clean work surface and shape pieces of dough into long, thin sausages. Cut into lengths of about 4 in/10 cm and press the ends of each length together to form a ring. ▪ Transfer the rings to a buttered and floured baking sheet. ▪ Bake in a preheated oven at 400°F/ 200°C/gas 6 for 25 minutes. ▪ Cool on a wire rack.

These simple and delicious little cookies are excellent to serve with coffee or tea.

Bigné di San Giuseppe

Lemon and egg fritters

Place the water, salt, butter, sugar, and lemon zest in a heavy-bottomed saucepan and bring to a boil. ▪ When the water is boiling, add the flour and stir with a wooden spoon. Continue cooking, stirring continuously, until the dough is thick and comes away from the sides of the saucepan. Remove from the heat and set aside to cool. ▪ When cool, stir in the eggs one at a time. The dough should be soft, but not runny. ▪ Set aside to rest for at least 1 hour. ▪ Heat the oil in a deep-sided skillet (frying pan) until very hot, but not smoking. ▪ Use a teaspoon to scoop up the dough and drop it into the hot oil. Fry the fritters, a few at a time, until they are plump and golden brown. ▪ Remove the fritters from the oil with a slotted spoon and drain on paper towels. Keep warm. Repeat until all the dough has been used up. ▪ Sprinkle with confectioners' sugar and serve hot.

Serves: 4–6
Preparation: 25 minutes + 1 hour's resting
Cooking: 25 minutes
Recipe grading: fairly easy

- 1 cup/250 ml water
- dash of salt
- ½ cup/125 g butter
- ¼ cup/50 g superfine/caster sugar
- finely grated zest of 1 lemon
- 1⅔ cups/250 g all-purpose/plain flour
- 8 large eggs
- 1–2 cups/250–500 ml olive oil, for frying
- confectioners'/icing sugar, for sprinkling

Suggested wine: a sweet white
(Orvieto Dolce)

These fritters are traditionally served on March 19 – St. Joseph's Day – but they are delicious all year round.

Pesche al forno

Stuffed baked peaches

Wash the peaches under cold running water. Dry well and cut them in half. ▪ Remove the pit (stone) and use a teaspoon to hollow out a hole about the size of a golf ball from the centers. ▪ Place the peach flesh in a bowl and add three-quarters of the amaretti cookies and all but 4 tablespoons of the sugar. Mix well and use the mixture to fill the peaches. ▪ Spread the butter over the bottom of an ovenproof dish large enough to hold all the peach halves quite snugly. Arrange the peaches in it. ▪ Drizzle with the rum and sprinkle with the remaining amaretti cookies and sugar. ▪ Bake in a preheated oven at 350°F/180°C/gas 4 for 30 minutes. ▪ Serve hot or warm.

Serves: 4–6
Preparation: 25 minutes
Cooking: 30 minutes
Recipe grading: fairly easy

- 4–6 large ripe peaches
- $3\frac{1}{2}$ oz/100 g amaretti cookies, crushed
- $\frac{3}{4}$ cup/150 g superfine/caster sugar
- 2 tablespoons butter
- 4 tablespoons dark rum

Suggested wine: a sweet dessert white
(Colli Albani Dolce Superiore)

The sweet almondy taste of the amaretti cookies blends perfectly with the peaches and rum. Use more or less sugar depending on how sweet you like it. These are excellent with whipped cream or ice cream.

Serves: 8–10
Preparation: 20 minutes
Cooking: 20 minutes
Recipe grading: easy

- 1 cup/125 g whole blanched almonds
- ¾ cup/150 g superfine/caster sugar
- ⅔ cup/100 g all-purpose/plain flour
- 4 tablespoons butter
- 1 teaspoon ground cinnamon
- 1 large egg
- grated zest of ½ lemon

Suggested wine: a sweet dessert wine
(Aleatico di Gradoli)

Fave dolci

Almond cookies

Spread the almonds in a large baking pan and toast in a preheated oven at 350°F/ 180°C/gas 4 for around 8 minutes, or until the almonds are just beginning to color. Remove from the oven and set aside to cool. ▪ Combine the cooled almonds with half the sugar in a food processor fitted with a steel blade. Process until the almonds are ground to a powder. ▪ Place the almonds and sugar in a mixing bowl and stir in three-quarters of the flour, the butter, the cinnamon, egg, and lemon zest. Mix well to obtain a smooth, firm dough. ▪ Use the remaining flour to lightly flour a clean work surface and shape the dough into a long sausage. Slice crosswise to obtain small, oval cookies. Sprinkle with the remaining sugar. ▪ Transfer the cookies to a greased and floured baking sheet and bake in a preheated oven at 300°F/150°C/gas 2 for 20 minutes, or until the cookies are light golden brown. ▪ Remove from the sheet and set aside to cool on a wire rack. After a few hours they will be crisp. Store in an airtight cookie jar.

These cookies are called "fave" (fava beans or broad beans) because of their shape. They are also called All Souls' Cookies because they are traditionally served in early November to celebrate the Roman Catholic feast day.

Acknowledgments

The Publishers would like to thank Mastrociliegia, Fiesole (Florence) who kindly lent props for photography.

All photos by Marco Lanza except:

Farabolafoto, Milan: 1, 2, 5, 6, 8, 9, 11t, 12 t, 13, 22t, 23, 41br, 47, 68l, 69, 84b, 85, 93tl;
Giuseppe Carfagna, Rome: 7b, 12b, 20t, 68r, 93br Adriano Nardi, Florence: 3, 11b;
Archivio Scala, Florence: 76; Overseas, Milan 41bl, 41t, 84t;
Illustrations: Ivan Stalio 92t, 93c, 93tr; Paola Ravaglia: 7